Exploring Theological English

TEACHER'S GUIDE

T0204649

Exploring Theological English

Reading, Vocabulary, and Grammar for ESL/EFL
TEACHER'S GUIDE

Cheri L. Pierson

Lonna J. Dickerson

Florence R. Scott

PIQUANT
editions

Copyright ©2010 by Cheri L. Pierson, Lonna J. Dickerson, and Florence R. Scott

The moral right of Cheri L. Pierson, Lonna J. Dickerson, and Florence R. Scott to be identified as the Authors of this Work has been asserted by them in accordance with the Copyright, Designs and Patents Act 1988.

First published in Great Britain in 2010 by Piquant Editions
PO BOX 83, Carlisle, CA3 9GR
www.piquanteditions.com

ISBN: 978-1-903689-41-7

All Rights Reserved.
No part of this book may be reproduced or transmitted in any form or by any means—electronic, mechanical, photocopying, recording, or any other—except for brief quotations in printed reviews, without the prior permission of the publisher.

British Library Cataloguing in Publication Data

Pierson, Cheri.
  Exploring theological English : reading, vocabulary, and
  grammar for ESL/EFL.
  Teacher's guide.
  1. English language--Religious aspects--Christianity--
  Study and teaching--Foreign speakers. 2. Theology--
  Terminology--Study and teaching.
  I. Title II. Dickerson, Lonna J., 1942- III. Scott,
  Florence R.
  428.2'4'071-dc22

Unless otherwise stated, all biblical quotations are taken from the Holy Bible, New International Version (NIV), Copyright 1973, 1978, 1984 by International Bible Society.

Cover design by Luzdesign (www.projectluz.com)
Book design by ToaTee (www.2at.com)

Contents

Unit C: Answer Key

Appendixes, Notes, and References

Companion Website for teachers and students:
www.ExploringTheologicalEnglish.com

Preface

Exploring Theological English: Teacher's Guide introduces teachers, tutors, and other readers to the field of English for Bible and Theology and argues for the need to help learners of English as a second language bridge the gap between the type of English that is used in everyday informal conversation and the specialized variety of the language that appears in more scholarly biblical and theological publications.

In a more ideal world, all people would have the opportunity to study the Word of God in their native language, and all Christians would have available a range of Bible study tools written in their own language—tools to help them grow in their faith and to share that faith with others. But this is not an ideal world. Even though at least a portion of the Bible has been translated into more than 2,400 different languages, few Bible study resources are available in most of these same languages. This means that large numbers of Christians, including thousands of students in Bible schools and seminaries around the world, must use another language—most often English—in order to gain access to the wealth of biblical and theological publications available. The paucity of resources in a large number of languages also means that Christian leaders from all corners of the world frequently come to English-speaking countries, such as the United States, Canada, and the United Kingdom, to pursue biblical studies in seminaries and graduate schools. Unfortunately, many of these individuals do not have the level of English proficiency required for tasks such as reading biblical journals and textbooks, taking course work, and communicating on a professional level with their colleagues in English. And even more troublesome, the teachers of many of these learners do not have the requisite preparation for designing and implementing an effective English program to upgrade the language skills of their students.

This *Teacher's Guide* provides practical help for these teachers. It discusses current issues and procedures related to teaching this specialized area of English as a second or foreign language (ESL/EFL) to native speakers of other languages. It addresses the practical needs of administrators and instructors in Bible institutes and seminaries, as well as educators in colleges and universities worldwide. It also provides valuable guidance for students who are preparing to teach English for Bible and Theology (EBT) and for teacher trainers in this discipline.

In writing this *Teacher's Guide*, we hope to reach a wider audience with the insights we have gained through teaching EBT and through training others to teach and develop materials in this specialized area of instruction. We have not only drawn upon our own experiences, but we have also dialogued with others who teach EBT at various locations around the world. In addition, we have conducted a series of needs analyses and collected a broad range of data from survey forms, personal interviews, and on-site visits to overseas locations where EBT instruction is part of the curriculum.

Companion Website for teachers and students:
www.ExploringTheologicalEnglish.com

Introduction

English for Bible and Theology

English for Bible and Theology (EBT): The teaching or learning of the specific variety of English used in Bible and theology classes, textbooks, and articles in these disciplines, sermons, etc. One subtype of EBT is **Theological English (TE),** which focuses on aspects of English related to the study of theology, including theological terms, the range of complex sentence structures used in theological writing, and even the broader organizational patterns used by theologians in their teaching and writing.

This introduction addresses some fundamental questions teachers and learners often ask about English for Bible and Theology (EBT): What is EBT? How does an EBT course differ from other English classes for those who are native speakers of other languages? What is the difference between EBT and Theological English (TE)? Is specialized instruction in English really needed in order to study theology? Why isn't a high level of language proficiency, plus a good dictionary, adequate for the learners' needs? How do EBT and TE courses differ from the range of Bible and theology courses found in seminaries and Bible institutes as well as in graduate and undergraduate Christian higher education? Before we discuss these questions, we need to define some acronyms used for different types of English courses.

Common Acronyms

ESL	**English as a Second Language:** English taught or learned in countries where it has an official status and is commonly used as the medium of general communication. These countries include the United States, Canada, the United Kingdom, South Africa, Australia, and New Zealand. ESL learners are often immigrants or refugees who plan to remain in the country or students who may return to their native countries after a period of study. Although we use the term *second language,* English may be the learners' third, fourth, or even tenth language.
EFL	**English as a Foreign Language:** English taught or learned in countries where English has no official status and is not commonly used as the medium of general communication, as the medium of academic instruction, or for other purposes such as government and media. For example, those who teach English in Russia, Turkey, and China teach English as a foreign language. Some authors and practitioners in the field blur the contrast between ESL and EFL. North Americans often use ESL as a generic acronym to refer to teaching English to native speakers of other languages regardless of the country or environment in which instruction takes place; in other parts of the world, the terms EFL and ELT (English Language Teaching) are preferred.
GPE	**General Purpose English:** Sometimes called General English (GE), this refers to the common core of language skills essential for learners from all disciplines.
ESP	**English for Specific Purposes:** The teaching or learning of the varieties of English used for specific professional or job-related tasks or skills (e.g., Business English, Medical English, English for Aviation, English for Banking). ESP includes both English for Academic Purposes and English for Occupational Purposes.
EAP	**English for Academic Purposes:** The teaching or learning of the varieties of English used in academic work (e.g., English for Bible and Theology).
EOP	**English for Occupational Purposes:** The teaching or learning of the varieties of English used in different professions (e.g., English for Engineers) and occupations (e.g., English for Tour Guides).

For a more complete list of terms and acronyms, see the following Web sites:
Institute for Cross-Cultural Training:
http://www.wheaton.edu/bgc/ICCT/ResandLinks/acronyms.html
The Internet TESL Journal: http://iteslj.org/acronyms.html

Types of English Courses

To illustrate where EBT courses fit into the larger context of ESL/EFL instruction, Figure I.1 provides a visual summary of the different categories and subcategories of classes, along with a few of the many possible courses in each category. It shows instruction categorized according to overall focus: General Purpose English (GPE) or English for Specific Purposes (ESP).

In addition, we can distinguish between two broad and often considerably overlapping categories of ESP, English for Academic Purposes (EAP) and English for Occupational Purposes (EOP). EAP courses are generally for students who are learning in a classroom or another academic setting, while EOP courses are usually for on-the-job workers with very specific and usually non-academic uses for English. Note that we have placed EBT in the EAP family. Because most students require this knowledge for academic purposes, we consider EBT to be a subcategory of EAP, not EOP. However, like nearly all other EAP courses, the EBT course content also has considerable value for those who are not studying in an academic context.

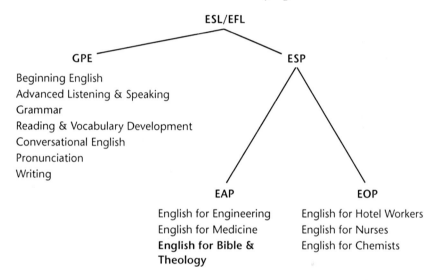

Figure I.1: Categories of ESL/EFL Teaching and Learning

General Purpose English (GPE). Regardless of their ultimate purpose for learning English, beginning ESL/EFL students tend to have many shared instructional needs. All learners require a basic knowledge of grammar and high frequency vocabulary. The majority also want to develop oral communication skills (proficiency in listening and speaking) as well as literacy skills (proficiency in reading and writing). These non-specialized needs can be met by instruction in General Purpose English. By choosing to focus broadly on the learners' shared English-language needs, we find that the ESL/EFL content and learning activities suitable for seminary students may differ little from the content and learning activities useful for medical workers, bankers, and those engaged in international trade. In fact, in many classrooms where GPE is taught, students represent a wide variety of contexts for their future use of the language. Furthermore, GPE courses may be offered at all levels (beginning, intermediate, advanced), in all skills (listening, speaking, reading, writing), and for all language components (e.g., vocabulary, grammar, pronunciation). While instruction for beginning and intermediate learners may cover all skills and components in a single course, high-intermediate and advanced classes frequently deal with only one or two skills (e.g., high intermediate reading, advanced listening and speaking) or components (e.g., advanced grammar, advanced pronunciation) or combinations of skills and components (e.g., high-intermediate reading and vocabulary development, advanced conversational English).[1]

English for Specific Purposes (ESP). Once they have reached the intermediate to high-intermediate level, most ESL/EFL students also use their newly acquired language skills beyond their English classroom. If they are working in a job or profession, communicating with co-workers about job-specific responsibilities is likely to require a command of specialized vocabulary and terms. If they are students, they may need English to read an article, listen to a lecture, watch a DVD, or attend a conference in which presentations are in English. Learners such as these have very specific purposes for using English. Their motivation is often the highest and their learning the most efficient when instruction takes into account the English-language subject areas they will need to deal with (e.g., theology, medicine, business) and the tasks they must carry out (e.g., reading textbooks, understanding academic lectures, dealing with medical patients, selling products internationally). Language teaching specialists categorize these courses under the rubric English for Specific Purposes. Hutchinson and Waters (1987, 19) define ESP as follows:

> ESP is not a particular kind of language or methodology, nor does it consist of a particular type of teaching material. Understood properly, it is an approach to language learning, which is based on learner need. The foundation of all ESP is the simple question: Why does this learner need to learn a foreign language? . . . ESP, then, is an approach to language teaching in which all decisions as to content and method are based on the learner's need for learning.

English for Bible and Theology (EBT). When their English-language needs include tasks such as reading theology textbooks, writing term papers about church history, participating in class discussions about biblical topics, and perhaps even teaching Bible studies or preaching, these learners can profit from the category of ESP that we call English for Bible and Theology. In particular, high-intermediate and advanced learners can usually progress more rapidly when materials and learning activities focus on (1) the content they will deal with in their Bible and theology course work (and for some, their future ministry), (2) the discipline-specific language they must master, and (3) the range of tasks they will need to handle in English.

Although learners can acquire their knowledge of EBT through self-study, many gain this expertise more easily through enrollment in a course or through individual tutoring. EBT courses are often more essential in an overseas context where English is not commonly spoken, but they are also valuable additions for international students in countries where English is the dominant language. Most international students who have not taken previous Bible and theology course work in English, including many who have used English as the medium of instruction in other courses, can profit from EBT instruction before or concurrently with their first Bible and/or theology course taught in English.

EBT is a broad category that encompasses a variety of courses related to the study of ESL/EFL and to the subject matter of the Bible and/or theology. Some EBT courses focus on areas that are not necessarily academic in nature, such as helping students learn common biblical terms, understand English sermons, or read the English Bible or Christian journal articles written for a lay audience. However, EBT classes usually deal with topics that are more academic, such as teaching the skills needed for reading theological publications, listening to lectures on biblical themes, discussing opposing theological viewpoints, or writing scholarly articles.

When students must do most or all of their Bible and theology course work in English, their EBT course should include all four skills: listening, speaking, reading, and writing. Even at the high-intermediate to advanced level, these same students will probably need to focus on content areas such as vocabulary, pronunciation, and grammar, and perhaps also learning strategies and other areas related to second language acquisition.

In many Bible schools and seminaries in an EFL context (i.e., where English is not the language of the wider community), students handle most of their learning activities in their native language. This includes listening to lectures, interacting with professors and colleagues, and writing papers. In many of these same institutions, however, only a small number of theological publications are available in the native language. Therefore, the school's library and the professors' reading lists may consist primarily of volumes written in English. To access this broad range of theological textbooks and journals, students must have at least a moderately strong reading knowledge of English. For these students, the optimal EBT course would be one that focuses primarily on the reading skill.

Theological English (TE) courses focus on the English-language needs of theology students, and they are generally quite academic in nature. Some students in TE classes can also profit from taking other EBT classes that focus on a variety of English skills as well as different types of biblical and theological content. Others may need only a Theological English class, and not the broader EBT instruction.

Exploring Theological English is a TE textbook that is primarily for those interested in studying theology in an academic context. Our English-language goal is to help learners develop their English skills in the areas of reading, theological and general academic vocabulary, and advanced grammatical structures. While we recognize that theology students may also want to focus on the other three language skills (listening, speaking, and writing), this textbook does not focus directly on those needs. Our theological goal is to introduce the range of topics and vocabulary found in most introductory theology textbooks.

The Need for Theological English Instruction

When discussing the need for Theological English (TE) instruction, teachers and administrators typically voice a range of opinions and concerns. Those who have not personally observed students having difficulties in using English for their theology studies may ask, "Do students really need specialized English instruction which focuses on this discipline? Isn't a good General Purpose English course sufficient preparation, especially if it's a course that emphasizes academic skills?" They may even mention students who do very well in their theology classes without the benefit of a TE course. We acknowledge that there are gifted learners who develop a high level of proficiency in English, and without specialized TE instruction they handle their theological studies quite well. These are the students, usually few in number, who somehow make it to the top of their classes in spite of having less-than-ideal formal language learning experiences. These, however, are usually not the typical learners; they are the exceptions. In addition, these same individuals often tell us that they could have reached more easily, or even exceeded, their present level of proficiency with the help of a TE course and a range of learning materials designed to meet their specialized needs.

Those who have observed students struggling with the English language may ask, "Why is it that the majority of my students have a horrendous time trying to make sense of reading assignments in our introductory theology textbook, but they can understand the same concepts when presented in their native language?" Or, "Can anything be done to help our students so that they won't have to spend ten hours poring over a single page of theology—and then not really understand what they have read?" Or, for classes comprised of native and non-native speakers, "I know Mr. Kim understands the theological arguments better than 90% of his classmates, including most of the native English speakers, but he seems to comprehend little from his reading assignments. What can I do to help him?"

Unfortunately, in many Christian institutions a large number of non-native English speakers struggle through their assignments and activities that require advanced English ability. They take longer to complete reading assignments, and their comprehension is often inadequate. They frequently rely on others for help with required assignments and they seldom do optional assignments that might enrich their learning. They tend to refrain from taking courses with extensive and/or difficult readings, and some fail to graduate, dropping out of school before completing their studies. These students desperately need the kind of instruction that will help them bridge the gap between what they learn in their GPE classes and the level and type of English required by their theology courses. Figure I.2 illustrates this gap between what students learn in their GPE classes and the English-language demands of their theology courses.

GPE → 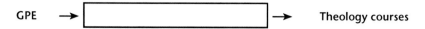 → **Theology courses**

Figure I.2: The Gap Between GPE Courses and Theology Courses

To explain in more detail the need for TE instruction, we will look first at two typical GPE classes taught in countries where English is not the primary language of instruction. Then we will focus on the English-language reading demands of a typical theology course with a textbook and other readings only in English. This will allow us to see more clearly the gap that exists between the instruction provided in even the best GPE courses and the English-language needs of theology students. Examining this gap can help us understand more fully why GPE classes fail to provide adequate preparation for most theology students and, in turn, help us recognize the contribution of courses designed to meet the reading goals of these students.

Although there can be dozens of types and subtypes of GPE classes, we will look at two fairly typical classes taught in overseas contexts. Each offers learning opportunities that help students grow in their English proficiency. However, neither provides the most effective preparation for students who must read theology materials in English.

A communicative GPE class. Moscow, Russia: 20 adults meeting for two semesters, three times per week for two hours per class. The prominence of grammar and vocabulary learning are less obvious in this communicative class in Moscow. Instead, the primary emphasis is on oral communication with students interacting verbally with the teacher, in small groups with other class members, and sometimes in pairs. The focus is on everyday language—the topics and typical phrases and sentences used when interacting informally with others. Homework varies from listening to a tape or CD-ROM and answering questions by writing short sentences to finding another person and practicing the dialogues or other oral content of the day's lesson. The second semester of this communicative curriculum differs from the first primarily in the complexity of language and the types of activities that students handle. For example, students often take part in group discussions, plan projects together, and watch television or movies.

Evaluation: This course is more appropriate for those who want to travel to English-speaking countries as tourists and those who wish to interact informally with English speakers in Russia. However, its lack of emphasis on reading and writing skills make it less desirable for those who need to use English for academic work. Bible and theology students who spend two semesters in this curriculum will find it exceedingly difficult to handle the demands of a theology course with a large number of reading assignments in English.

A traditional GPE class. Warsaw, Poland: 25 young adults meeting for two years, twice a week for two hours per class. Primary emphasis is placed on the learning of grammar and general-purpose vocabulary. Classroom activities generally consist of explanation of grammar points followed by sentence-level pencil-and-paper exercises (e.g., fill in the blank, short answer, multiple choice), memorization of vocabulary lists (often supplied by the teacher), and occasional translation of sentences from one language to the other. Oral work consists mainly of going over the written homework exercises. Reading and writing assignments tend to deal with sentences and short paragraphs. Most students rely heavily on their bilingual English-Polish dictionaries.

Evaluation: While it is important for students to learn English grammar and general vocabulary, courses such as this one often cover far too many grammar points with far too little practice. Students frequently finish two years of English with little ability to actually use the language and often with low motivation to continue learning. After completing this traditional curriculum, some students can read most basic biblical resources, especially when they have dealt with similar subject matter in their native language. Most, however, find even two years of English to be inadequate for their needs. While these students have learned a great many vocabulary words and have practiced their reading skills, they have not dealt with vocabulary or topics similar to those found in the Bible or theological materials. These learners are generally unprepared to handle the activities and tasks in a typical theology class.

While these two English classes can be of value to many different types of language learners, neither provides the optimal match for theology students who must handle reading activities and tasks such as those listed in Figure I.3. For these learners, instruction in GPE—when it excludes any work in EBT and especially TE—is not the most efficient approach to language learning because it requires devoting large blocks of time to the mastery of content that often has little value for the students' personal and professional goals. When time and effort are given to content and activities of lesser value—even when essential skills such as reading are emphasized—more important needs are neglected and the learners often lose motivation to study English. Furthermore, without help for their specialized needs, even many of those who have attained a high level of proficiency in GPE may have difficulty in handling highly technical discipline-specific tasks, such as reading theology textbooks with a moderate to high level of comprehension. Therefore, for optimal success in second language acquisition, as well as their subject-matter discipline, we believe that intermediate to advanced students will learn more efficiently and maintain higher motivation when at least some of their classroom instruction or individual tutoring is geared to the specialized uses of the language.

Bridging the Gap Between GPE Instruction and Theology Courses

The primary purpose of TE instruction is to prepare learners for the English-language requirements of theology courses. This is accomplished by bridging the gap (Figure I.2) between what students have learned in GPE classes and what will be required of them in their theological studies. More specifically, TE courses are designed (1) to bridge the gap between the generic content common to most GPE courses—topics of general interest and usefulness to all students—and the content of theology courses and (2) to sharpen the students' learning skills, such as reading and vocabulary development, that are essential for their academic course work. The precise focus of each TE class should differ, depending on the English-language content and language-learning skills required of that particular group of learners in their theological studies.

Theology courses. The primary purpose of theology courses differs considerably from that of Theological English courses. Theology courses are designed to involve students in the discipline of theology so that "they acquire a deeper understanding of the subject matter and can formulate a biblically based, historically informed, reasonably consistent, and contemporaneously meaningful statement of a Christian worldview" (personal communication with J. Julius Scott, Jr., Professor Emeritus of Biblical and Historical Studies at Wheaton College Graduate School).

Figure I.3 highlights the similarities and contrasts between these two types of courses: a TE course, *English for Theology: Reading and Vocabulary Development,* and an introductory theology course, *Christian Doctrines.* An examination of the goals, learning materials, and sample learning activities for the two courses shows that they differ in each of the three categories on the chart. Although Figure I.3 shows that there is some overlap between the two courses, the primary focus of the TE course is on English language skills while the major emphasis of the Christian Doctrines course is on theology. For example, the most basic goal for the theological English students is the development of language skills related to reading, while a more advanced goal is the application of these skills to the learning of key theological concepts and vocabulary. On the other hand, the Christian Doctrines course assumes learners are beginning their studies with the requisite English skills for accomplishing each of the four goals listed in Figure I.3. In this course, learners must first understand broad theological themes. After that, they go beyond this basic goal to three others that involve the application of this newly acquired knowledge to a range of practical issues Christians face in their daily lives.

	English for Theology: Reading and Vocabulary Development	Christian Doctrine
Goals	• develop language skills needed to read theology books and articles written in English • learn key concepts and vocabulary used in theology books and articles written in English	• understand the normative themes of Christian theological literature • address concerns regarding the relevance of Christian theology • encourage genuine convictions concerning the Christian faith • acquire a better understanding of the role of Christian theology in the church
Learning Materials	• variety of exercises to develop reading and vocabulary skills • readings (often simplified) that deal with key concepts and terms • two English Bibles (one translation that is a literal or formal equivalent, one that is a functional or dynamic equivalent)	• Bible • theology textbook(s) and articles
Sample Learning Activities	• use available clues to determine meaning (e.g., context, grammatical structures, graphic symbols) • identify main idea and supporting details • scan passage for specific information • use English-only theological dictionary	• complete reading assignments • listen to class lectures and take notes • participate in class discussions • write a critical review of a chapter from a required textbook • write your personal doctrinal statement • take two written examinations

Figure I.3: Contrasts Between EBT and Theology Courses

Four Typical Sequences for EBT and/or TE Instruction

Figure I.4 illustrates four typical instructional sequences that provide effective preparation for the study of Bible and theology in English. Although some students may take only one GPE course, most will take a number of courses. While EBT and/or TE may be a single course, we prefer to have two separate courses so that students can begin with more general EBT instruction and then focus on TE with its more challenging concepts as well as its more complex English-language demands. Also, in some situations teachers may wish to focus on listening and speaking skills in an

EBT course and then put more emphasis on reading (and perhaps writing) in the TE course.

Figure I.4: Four Typical Sequences for EBT Instruction

Note that in Figure I.4 all sequences begin with General Purpose English (GPE). These courses are usually for beginning and intermediate to high-intermediate learners. Ideally, students would be at least at the high-intermediate level before studying EBT and/or TE, as this promotes an easier transition into the study of biblical and theological materials. However, we recognize that many students do not have the time nor opportunity to gain a moderate to high level of proficiency in the language before they begin their biblical and theological studies in English.

1. Schedule 1 allows learners to continue their study of GPE while also focusing on EBT and/or TE. This is often the approach that is most beneficial for those who have studied English for only a short time (e.g., 1-4 years), as it encourages these students to continue advancing in their weaker areas of GPE while also beginning their study of EBT and/or TE. This is usually the ideal sequence for Bible schools and seminaries in countries where English is not the primary language of instruction for all levels of education, beginning with the elementary grades.

2. Schedule 2 is usually most appropriate for those who have studied GPE for several years. This sequence can provide a good foundation in EBT and/or TE, making an easier transition for beginning the study of theology. It is usually appropriate for students who have been required to earn a high score on an English proficiency test, such as the TOEFL or IELTS,[2] in order to be admitted to a college or university where all instruction is in English. It may also be the most ideal approach for students who have studied other subjects in English and for those who have only a short time (e.g., a few weeks or months) to study EBT and/or TE before beginning a Bible and theology curriculum.

3. Schedule 3 can be a useful approach for learners with strong English skills—ideally those who are high-intermediate to advanced learners in GPE and perhaps have also taken other courses in English. This approach may also be appropriate for those who anticipate that their study of Bible and theology will be challenging either because they have occasional difficulties with English or because they are not familiar with the English terms and concepts

used in these disciplines. For students who do not already have at least moderately strong English skills, Schedule 3 can work successfully only when the biblical and theological content is presented in simplified English or when the student's native language is used for part of the instruction.

4. Schedule 4 is ideal for advanced learners who need to give some attention to one area of GPE, such as pronunciation or writing skills, yet they generally have sufficiently strong English skills for studying EBT and/or TE and a limited amount of Bible and theology. In addition, this approach is often appropriate for those who need some individual or small-group tutoring in English in order to keep up with classmates who have more advanced English skills. We do not recommend Schedule 4 for those who do not have at least moderately strong skills in GPE.

Conclusion

Each year more biblical and theological materials are published in English than in any other language. No matter which country our students come from or which language they speak natively, most non-native speakers of English find it moderately challenging to exceedingly difficult to read theological publications written for native English speakers. The goal of our student textbook, *ETE*, is to make this task easier by giving learners the kind of instruction they need in order to bridge the gap between their current command of the English language and the very specific language demands placed on them as they seek to comprehend theological articles and books written in English. The goal of our *Teacher's Guide* is to provide you as the instructor with the kind of help you need in order to teach *ETE* more effectively. This includes addressing the need for EBT and TE instruction, helping you in planning and implementing instruction that is appropriate for your students' needs, and giving chapter-by-chapter teaching suggestions and an answer key for all exercises.

Unit A

Preparing to Teach

Exploring Theological English

Before you teach *ETE* for the first time, we suggest that you read through this unit, which will guide you in answering three key questions:

1. How can you determine if *ETE* is at the right reading level for your students?

   Before teaching *ETE*, you will need to know if your students are likely to face so many challenges in reading comprehension that they will either not be able to use the book at this time or they will require an excessive amount of time and/or assistance in order to do the readings. Part I provides an easy-to-use test for determining your learners' level of reading readiness. It also discusses test administration, scoring, and interpretation.

2. How can you adapt *ETE* to meet student needs?

   No textbook will be right in every way for the individual needs of each of your students. This means you should plan to adapt the materials in one or more ways. You may need to modify the difficulty level, making it easier or more challenging. You may need to modify the quantity and/or type of material, either omitting or adding some exercises or sections. Part II provides practical suggestions for adapting *ETE* so that it will be appropriate for the students in your class.

3. How does *ETE* prepare learners for reading theological publications?

   To become good readers—those who can read at an appropriate pace while understanding and remembering what they are reading— requires some basic knowledge and skills that nearly every ESL/EFL student needs to learn and practice. Part III provides an overview of the three types of learning experiences *ETE* uses to equip learners to become more proficient readers: reading skills, vocabulary skills, and grammar skills.

PART I: Determining if *ETE* is at the Right Level

Essential to the successful teaching of *ETE* is ensuring that the readings are at a level that your learners can comprehend without having to make extensive use of a dictionary. An easy-to-administer technique for determining reading level is the *cloze procedure* or *cloze test*, which requires students to begin with a passage from which words have been systematically deleted (e.g., every seventh to tenth word is missing). The students' task is to analyze the passage and fill in each blank with what they believe to be the most appropriate word choice. They supply the missing word based on contextual clues (e.g., sentence structure, part of speech, vocabulary) and their knowledge of the subject matter.

Before you begin to teach *ETE*, we suggest that you administer the two cloze tests in this *Teacher's Guide*. The results can help you determine whether *ETE* is at an appropriate level for your class as a whole, and then you can make the necessary adjustments. (See pp. 12-18 for adapting *ETE* for students at lower or higher levels.) Because most classes will be made up of students with different levels of reading ability, the cloze test can also help you identify individual students for whom you need to make further adjustments because their level is considerably higher or lower than most others in the class. In addition, if you are working with a large number of students, the cloze scores can help you divide learners into smaller groups based on their level of reading ability.

Cloze Reading Passages

There are two cloze reading passages provided in this section of the *Teacher's Guide* (pp. 7-8). You may photocopy these for use with your students. We recommend that you use both passages before you begin teaching *ETE*. They are not equal in difficulty and will give different results. When we pre-tested these two passages with our students, we found that Reading B was more difficult for everyone in our sample test group. Therefore, using the two readings, rather than one, will provide a more accurate picture of your students' ability to handle the *ETE* readings. Also, by beginning with Reading A for every other student and Reading B for the others, you can minimize the sharing of answers during the test administration.

Each reading passage is approximately 250-300 words with about 30 blanks to fill in. The missing words have been selected to represent a range of difficulty, and they include content words (nouns, adjectives, verbs, and adverbs) and function words (articles, prepositions, and conjunctions).

Administering the Cloze

1. Assure students that they will not receive a grade for their performance on the cloze procedure.

2. Explain the purpose, which is to help you learn more about their ability to comprehend theological materials so that you can adapt your instruction to their needs.
3. Make sure they understand the directions. To do this, you might want to use a short sample exercise, such as the following paragraph.

> According to the testimony of Scripture, God never changes. He is not subject to any process (1) _____ development. He can neither increase nor (2) _____. God's nature does not change because (3) _____ is already perfect. He is faithful (4) _____ his promises, and we can entrust (5) _____ souls to a faithful Creator. The (6) _____ character of God is often referred (7) _____ as immutability. Speaking of Christ, the writer to the Hebrews insists that he is "the same yesterday, today, and forever" (13:8).

Answers: (1) of, (2) decrease, (3) he, (4) to, (5) our, (6) unchanging, (7) to

4. Encourage them to write legibly.
5. Once they begin the cloze procedure, they should not be allowed to ask questions.
6. Give as much time as students need to complete the test.

Scoring the Cloze

An answer key is provided for each of the passages so that the scoring can be done easily and quickly (pp. 9-12.) You can score the test in two different ways: the easier method requires an exact word response while the second allows any word that is appropriate for the context and is also a synonym for the exact word. We suggest that you use both types of scoring. For the first, assign one point for each word that is identical to the word in the reading. If the word is misspelled but recognizable, give full credit. If it is not recognizable due to misspelling or poor handwriting, do not give any credit for the answer.

For the second method, determine which of the student answers are suitable equivalents for the exact word. (You may wish to consult with others in order to determine the words you will accept as synonyms. We have listed some acceptable equivalents in the answer key. However, your students may come up with additional acceptable equivalents.) Give one point for each appropriate word choice that has the same meaning as the correct answer. For example, in the sample paragraph above, the exact word for (6) is *unchanging*. But if students write *changeless* or *unchangeable*, we suggest that you give them full credit. You may also want to accept other close synonyms such as *stable, consistent, unvarying*. However, you should not accept a word that carries a meaning different from that of the exact word, nor should you accept a word that changes the meaning of the sentence, even when the substitute word makes sense in the context. For example, if a student writes the word *all* for (5) in the sample paragraph above, you should not accept this response because it does not carry the same meaning as the word *our*. Once you have determined the number of equivalent words you will accept as correct, add that number to the exact word score, thus giving a total of four scores for each student (two scores per student for each of the two reading passages). In nearly every case, the students' scores will be considerably higher when equivalent words are allowed. However, no one will be likely to achieve a perfect score—not even a native English speaker.

Interpreting Cloze Scores

By administering the two cloze tests in this section of the *Teacher's Guide*, you can usually identify the students with the strongest ability in reading comprehension and those who need the most help. But comparing students with one another does not tell you if even your strongest readers have sufficient command of English to be successful in using *ETE*. This requires additional interpretation of the cloze test scores. To help determine how well your students may be able to handle the *ETE* reading passages, use the chart in Figure A.1, which places learners into three broad ability levels: independent reading level, instructional reading level, and frustration reading level.

Independent reading level. Students who are operating at an independent reading level are likely to need some assistance from the teacher. They will usually be able to ask specific questions about content that they do not understand. For example, those who score at least 65% (exact word scoring) on Reading A and at least 40% (exact word scoring) on Reading B should be able to read the selections in *ETE* without much assistance from the instructor. However, this does not mean that they can read at the same rate or with the same level of understanding common to native English speakers.

Instructional reading level. Students who are operating at an instructional reading level are able to handle the content but will need more assistance— often considerable assistance—from the teacher. (See pp. 13–16 for suggestions for teaching *ETE* to learners who need considerable help.)

Frustration reading level. Students who are operating at a frustration reading level include those who require an excessive amount of assistance (generally those who are at the high end of the frustration level) all the way down to those who find the reading almost impossible to read (generally those at the low end of the frustration level). (See pp. 13–16 for suggestions for adapting *ETE* for learners who are at a lower proficiency level.)

	Reading A		Reading B	
	Exact Word Scoring	Acceptable Equivalent Scoring	Exact Word Scoring	Acceptable Equivalent Scoring
Independent Level	65–100%	75–100%	40–100%	50–100%
Instructional Level	55–64%	65–74%	30–39%	40–49%
Frustration Level	0–54%	0–64%	0–29%	0–39%

Figure A.1: Suggested Reading Levels Based on Cloze Tests

As you continue to administer these cloze tests to additional groups of students, you will find it easier to determine acceptable ranges of scores for your students. For example, for exact word scoring of Reading A, you may find that your students who score between 65–70% should be in the instructional level, not the independent level. Or for acceptable equivalent scoring of Reading A, you may find that students with scores of 55% should be considered to be at the instructional level, not the frustration level. Furthermore, after you have used *ETE* with two or three groups of students, you will know more about how to adapt the textbook and/or use other teaching procedures to prepare your students to read theological writing.

Those reading at the independent level can theoretically score 100% on the two cloze tests, but that is very unlikely for even your best students. When we used Reading A with our ESL students, the highest score was 76% for exact word scoring and 90% for acceptable equivalent scoring. For Reading B, the highest score was 50% for exact word scoring and 73% for acceptable equivalent scoring.

As part of your analysis of the cloze results, we suggest examining the items that were difficult for your students, noting the kinds of mistakes they made. This will help you anticipate future challenges and it can offer information about additional types of instruction you may need to provide.

Creating Additional Cloze Tests

If you want to create additional cloze exercises, we suggest the following steps.

1. Choose a passage from *ETE* that is approximately 250–300 words. The passage should make sense on its own and should not include a large number of proper names (names of specific people or places), uncommon terms or vocabulary, and/or a lot of quoted material (e.g., long passages enclosed in quotation marks).
2. Type out the passage as a double-spaced document.
3. Leave the title and first sentence intact. You may also want to leave the last sentence intact. Beginning with the second sentence, leave out every seventh to tenth word, depending on how difficult you

want to make the test. If the word to be deleted is a proper noun (e.g., a name or a person or place), a number, or a technical term that the student would have no knowledge of, choose the next possible word for deletion.

4. Make blanks for the missing words that are about 15 spaces in length—long enough for students to write the word in the blank. All blanks should be the same length.

5. Number each blank for scoring. There should be approximately 30 blanks in the passage.

6. Include clear written instructions on the same page as the cloze exercise.

7. Before you use your cloze passage with your class, do one or more trial runs with other groups or with a number of individuals. For example, you might have one of your colleagues from another school try out the test with his/her students, you might use it with a group of students at a higher proficiency level, and/or you might even want to try it out with native English speakers. The scores from each of these groups can give you valuable information. For example, in doing a trial run with Readings A and B, we found that Reading B was more difficult for every person in our test group, including native English speakers. For this reason, we suggested a different scale for the three levels (independent, instructional, frustration).

8. Depending on the difficulty of the reading, raise or lower the percentages required for the three reading levels.

9. Follow the same procedures described previously for administering, scoring, and interpreting your cloze test.

Reading A   Name _____

Directions
- *Read the entire passage quickly.*
- *Read each sentence slowly, and in each blank write one word that you believe correctly fills the blank.*
- *Read the entire passage again to make sure that your answers make sense.*
- *Fill every blank with a word, even if you have to guess at the answer.*

Humans in Their Initial Created State

According to the Bible, to be human is to be made "in the image of God." It
(1) _____ this expression that distinguished or separated humanity from
(2) _____ other creatures. In spite of its significance, we are never
(3)_____ precisely what the phrase "image of God" means.
(4) _____ the history of the church, many have undertaken
(5) _____ define and interpret its meaning. Some have suggested
(6) _____ God's image is something present in the makeup
(7) _____ humans. This has been interpreted by some to
(8) _____ the ability of humans to think and reason. (9) _____
have equated it with the human soul. To (10) _____ made in God's
image has also been explained (11) _____ terms of the relationship
experienced with God or (12) _____ other humans. This idea is
sometimes based on (13) _____ teaching of the relationship within
the Godhead itself, (14) _____ God is triune. The "image of God,"
therefore, (15) _____ be considered a relational quality. Others have
accounted (16) _____ it in terms of human function, such as
(17) _____ responsibility given by God to humankind to exercise
(18) _____ over creation (Gen 1:26–30).

There are implications for this (19) _____ principle. An obvious one is an
understanding that (20) _____ belong to God. He is our Creator and
(21) _____ made us to be in a right relationship (22) _____
himself. We are also made for relationship with (23) _____ other, with
the rest of creation, and even (24) _____ ourselves. Moreover, the
statement tells us that every (25) _____ being is valuable. For example,
murder was prohibited (26) _____ the grounds that humans were made
in the (27) _____ of God (Gen 9:6). It should likewise be noted
(28) _____ being made in the image of God is (29) _____
universal characteristic of humankind.

Reading B   Name _____

Directions
- *Read the entire passage quickly.*
- *Read each sentence slowly, and in each blank write one word that you believe correctly fills the blank.*
- *Read the entire passage again to make sure that your answers make sense.*
- *Fill every blank with a word, even if you have to guess at the answer.*

Revelation

During his second missionary journey Paul found himself in the great city of Athens. Viewing firsthand its high level of (1) _____ and culture, he surveyed a (2) _____ which was also wholly dedicated to the (3) _____ of false gods. He began (4) _____ with the citizens of Athens, people whose (5) _____ pastime was to discuss and listen to (6) _____ ideas. Their interest grew as Paul (7) _____ them about Jesus who had (8) _____ from the dead. Wanting to hear more, (9) _____ invited Paul to a meeting of (10) _____ Areopagus, which had been established to oversee (11) _____ and moral matters.

Before this pagan (12) _____, one not yet acquainted with the God (13) _____ Israel and the Hebrew (14) _____, Paul began his address, "I see that in every (15) _____ you Athenians are very religious" (Acts 17:22). Evidence of this was (16) _____ many altars. Among them (17) _____one inscribed "TO AN UNKNOWN GOD." He continued, "Now what you worship as something unknown I am going to proclaim to you" (17:23).

Paul proceeded (18) _____ proclaim the living and true God (19) _____ has made himself known. This God is the personal (20) _____ who made the world and everything in it and the (21) _____ Designer who left nothing to chance. (22) _____ of God has been displayed to (23) _____ people through his works and his (24) _____ of creation. Yet sin and idolatry (25) _____ impaired both human capacity and the (26) _____to know God. God in his (27) _____ has been patient with human ignorance. (28) _____ now there is no excuse for human (29) _____, because the full revelation has been (30) _____ in the advent and work of Jesus Christ. This (31) _____who created and sustains all is the (32) _____God who will judge all. He will one day, by this same Jesus, judge the world with righteousness. He has given assurance of this to all people by raising him from the dead.

Cloze Answer Keys

Reading A: Humans in Their Initial Created State

According to the Bible, to be human is to be made "in the image of God." It (1) is this expression that distinguished or separated humanity from (2) all other creatures. In spite of its significance, we are never (3) told precisely what the phrase "image of God" means. (4) Throughout the history of the church, many have undertaken (5) to define and interpret its meaning. Some have suggested (6) that God's image is something present in the makeup (7) of humans. This has been interpreted by some to (8) mean the ability of humans to think and reason. (9) Others have equated it with the human soul. To (10) be made in God's image has also been explained (11) in terms of the relationship experienced with God or (12) with other humans. This idea is sometimes based on (13) the teaching of the relationship within the Godhead itself, (14) that God is triune. The "image of God," therefore, (15) might be considered a relational quality. Others have accounted (16) for it in terms of human function, such as (17) the responsibility given by God to humankind to exercise (18) dominion over creation (Gen 1:26–30).

There are implications for this (19) biblical principle. An obvious one is an understanding that (20) we belong to God. He is our Creator and (21) he made us to be in a right relationship (22) with himself. We are also made for relationship with (23) each other, with the rest of creation, and even (24) with ourselves. Moreover, the statement tells us that every (25) human being is valuable. For example, murder was prohibited (26) on the grounds that humans were made in the (27) image of God (Gen 9:6). It should likewise be noted (28) that being made in the image of God is (29) a universal characteristic of humankind.
(284 words)

Item Number	Exact Word	Acceptable Equivalent
1	is	
2	all	the
3	told	
4	Throughout	In, During
5	to	
6	that	
7	of	
8	mean	signify, explain
9	Others	Some
10	be	
11	in	

12	with	
13	the	a
14	that	
15	might	should, can
16	for	
17	the	
18	dominion	authority, power, stewardship
19	biblical	theological, important, basic
20	we	humans, they
21	he	
22	with	
23	each	
24	with	
25	human	
26	on	
27	image	
28	that	
29	a	the, one

Reading B: Revelation

During his second missionary journey Paul found himself in the great city of Athens. Viewing firsthand its high level of (1) civilization and culture, he surveyed a (2) city which was also wholly dedicated to the (3) worship of false gods. He began (4) talking with the citizens of Athens, people whose (5) favorite pastime was to discuss and listen to (6) new ideas. Their interest grew as Paul (7) told them about Jesus who had (8) risen from the dead. Wanting to hear more, (9) they invited Paul to a meeting of (10) the Areopagus, which had been established to oversee (11) religious and moral matters.

Before this pagan (12) audience, one not yet acquainted with the God (13) of Israel and the Hebrew (14) prophets, Paul began his address, "I see that in every (15) way you Athenians are very religious" (Acts 17:22). Evidence of this was (16) their many altars. Among them (17) was one inscribed "TO AN UNKNOWN GOD." He continued, "Now what you worship as something unknown I am going to proclaim to you" (17:23).

Paul proceeded (18) to proclaim the living and true God (19) who has made himself known. This God is the personal (20) Creator who made the world and everything in it and the (21) <u>great</u> Designer who left nothing to chance. (22) <u>Knowledge</u> of God has been displayed to (23) <u>all</u> people through his works and his (24) <u>care</u> of creation. Yet sin and idolatry (25) <u>have</u> impaired both human capacity and the (26) <u>desire</u> to know God. God in his (27) <u>mercy</u> has been patient with human ignorance. (28) <u>But</u> now there is no excuse for human (29) <u>ignorance,</u> because the full revelation has been (30) <u>given</u> in the advent and work of Jesus Christ. This (31) <u>God</u> who created and sustains all is the (32) <u>same</u> God who will judge all. He will one day, by this same Jesus, judge the world with righteousness. He has given assurance of this to all the people by raising him from the dead. (**314 words**)

Item Number	Exact Word	Acceptable Equivalent
1	civilization	society
2	city	temple, shrine
3	worship	
4	talking	speaking, debating, conversing
5	favorite	main, national, primary, normal
6	new	different, innovative
7	told	taught
8	risen	
9	they	
10	the	
11	religious	ethical, spiritual
12	audience	crowd, society, assembly
13	of	
14	prophets	scriptures
15	way	
16	their	
17	was	
18	to	
19	who	
20	Creator	God
21	great	wise, divine, almighty, ultimate
22	Knowledge	power, proof, evidence
23	all	

24	care	love
25	have	
26	desire	willingness, ability
27	mercy	grace, love
28	But	So
29	ignorance	
30	given	revealed, proclaimed, shown
31	God	
32	same	very, true

PART II: Adapting *ETE* to Meet Student Needs

ETE will probably not be at exactly the right proficiency level for each of your students. Even if it is at the right level, it might not have the precise focus you believe is best for your learners. Because of one or more of these differences, you will need to make modifications in your instruction.

- Your students may find the theological readings to be too difficult.
- Your students may find the theological exercises to be too difficult.
- Your students may need additional work on one or more aspects of *ETE*, such as the grammar exercises.
- Your students may need to develop English skills not addressed in *ETE*, such as listening comprehension and note taking, making oral presentations, writing papers, and/or informal conversation.
- Your students may not need to focus on one or more aspects of *ETE*, such as the grammar exercises.
- You may not have enough weeks or months to cover all of the chapters or sufficient class time to help your students work through the material.

To meet the specific needs of your students and to make the best use of your class time, you will probably find that you must adapt the textbook in one or more ways. In addition, you will need to add some supplementary instruction geared to the special needs of your students. But how do you know where to begin? We suggest that before teaching *ETE* you take the following five steps to discover more about your learners' needs:

1. Ask your students about the areas in which they need the most help. You may want to provide a checklist similar to the one in Appendix 2 (pp. 116–117). If you are teaching a group of students, you can usually get a more complete picture of their felt needs by

first using a checklist and then holding a class discussion to talk about their responses.

2. Talk with your students' future theology professors. Ask about the challenges faced by previous students with similar backgrounds in English. If your ESL students are currently enrolled in Bible and theology classes, learn as much as you can about their strengths, weaknesses, and special needs. Ask for suggestions about what to include in your English instruction in order to prepare your learners for success in their theology classes.

3. Examine the theology materials (e.g., articles, textbooks) that your students will use for each class. Find out which materials they will study first. For each class (or for each set of materials), note the areas that are likely to be most challenging as well as least challenging. Then look at the Contents section of *ETE* and also a few of the chapters to see how well this textbook prepares learners for their theology reading. Determine where you may need to supplement the *ETE* text, and also identify sections in the text that may not be as essential for your learners' needs.

4. For the relevant theology courses, examine course syllabi, assignments, and if possible, quizzes and major tests. Talk with the professors (and students, if appropriate) about the special challenges of ESL students. Ask to see samples of work done by ESL students. Then draw upon your findings as you plan how to supplement your *ETE* instruction with practice activities that allow your students to deal with the types of assignments, quizzes, and tests they will encounter in their theology courses.

5. If possible, visit your students' future (or current) theology classes. Identify the English-language requirements placed upon the students and observe how well they do in meeting those challenges. Then determine where you will need to provide instruction to help bridge the gap between your students' current level of language ability and what is required in their theology classes.

What can you do if your students are at a lower proficiency level?

Students at a somewhat lower proficiency level. For students who found the cloze tests (pp. 7-8) to be somewhat challenging (i.e., their scores were at the instructional level), we suggest that you take the following steps:

1. Determine more precisely your students' English-language needs— the areas they find most challenging: grammar and sentence structure, reading skills, academic vocabulary, and/or general vocabulary. Learning all you can about their specific challenges will help you provide instruction that is tailored to their areas of greatest need.

2. Examine your students' work habits and level of motivation. Make sure they understand that studying English for a given number

of months or years does not necessarily give them sufficient proficiency to handle the English-language demands of their theology courses. In their English classes, their aim should not be simply to pass the course, but to gain the language skills they need for their studies.

3. Find out as much as you can about how well your students use the reading and vocabulary strategies in the Introduction and Chapter 1 of *ETE*. For example, when reading English, do they guess at the meaning of some words and try to figure out their meanings from the context, or do they insist on looking up every new word in their dictionary? Are they willing to postpone learning the meanings of some new words, or do they insist on memorizing the meaning of every new word regardless of its importance? Depending on the importance of what they are reading, do they read some material more quickly, or do they always labor over each word in a paragraph? Once you discover your students' most serious challenges in mastering good reading and vocabulary habits, be sure to incorporate appropriate instruction into your English classes.

4. Assess factors such as the amount of student time required for their other courses, as well as other demands on your students' time and energy. While it is not always possible to make a great many changes in their overall learning programs or in their personal schedules, work with your students, the instructors, and others to make as many helpful adjustments as possible.

5. Supplement your *ETE* instruction with additional work in your students' most challenging areas, such as academic vocabulary development. You can find a short list of suggested ESL/EFL resources (books and Internet sites) in *ETE*, Appendix 4, pp. 357–361, and an additional list in Appendix 4 of the *Teacher's Guide (TG)*, pp. 126–133.

6. Depending on their specific needs, you may want to proceed more slowly in your work with *ETE* in order for your students to gain a stronger foundation in General Purpose English.

7. If your students are experiencing a number of English-language challenges, you may need to form small groups based on their specific needs, or you may be able to provide out-of-class tutoring for some individuals.

Students at a much lower proficiency level. For students who found the cloze tests to be exceedingly difficult (i.e., their scores were at the frustration level), implement as many of the seven steps listed above, as appropriate. In addition, do as many of the following as possible:

1. Postpone your *ETE* instruction until your students have a higher level of proficiency in General Purpose English (GPE). Consider requiring a minimum score on an English proficiency test before students are allowed to begin their biblical and/or theological courses that demand a high level of English proficiency.[1] This is a

common practice in many institutions where at least moderately strong English ability is required for academic success. See Appendix 4 (*TG*, pp. 126-133) for books and other materials to use for classroom instruction and tutoring.

2. Use the Vocabulary Levels Test[2] to determine your students' knowledge of vocabulary found in the 2,000 high-frequency word families of the *General Service List (GSL)*.[3]

3. Make sure your students learn the high-frequency English vocabulary in the *GSL*. (See *TG* Appendix 3, pp. 118-125.) Language teaching professionals such as Nation (2001, 16) insist on the mastery of these words before learners are allowed to focus on academic vocabulary (e.g., the Coxhead Academic Word List), technical or discipline-specific vocabulary (e.g., theological vocabulary), and low-frequency words.[4, 5]

4. Work with your students to develop basic reading skills, using the reading and vocabulary strategies listed in the Introduction and Chapter 1 of *ETE*. Begin by selecting one or two strategies that you believe are most important for your students and give them practice using these strategies before you move on to one or two additional strategies.

5. Before your students officially begin to study *ETE*, gradually introduce some of the academic vocabulary found in the textbook, or even a number of the more common theological terms.[6]

6. If you must begin using *ETE* before your students have a sufficiently high level of English proficiency, try to find materials on the same topics in the students' native language. Look for short articles or other information they can read before they tackle related readings in English. When your students have read related information in their native language, giving them an overall framework for understanding the content of a reading—that is, when they know generally what the reading is going to be about—usually they will be much more successful in understanding the content in English and remembering what they have read. While you should refrain from its overuse, some judicious use of the native language can help learners make more rapid progress in their learning of English.

7. In their native language, provide a short summary of the material to be read in English. This may be a written summary or an oral summary given by a classmate or another person. If you also speak the students' native language, this may be the ideal place to use their language in order to help them progress more quickly in their understanding of the theological concepts.

If your students need considerable work in GPE, you may be tempted to have them move directly from GPE instruction to their regular theology classes, skipping *ETE* altogether. While this might seem like a way to save time, your students will be more successful in reading English theological materials if they have *ETE* instruction before they are required to read theological materials in English. Keep in mind that while *ETE* may be challenging for your students, it is much less demanding than reading almost any theology book written in English and, can therefore be a highly useful tool for equipping your students for success in their theological studies.

What can you do if you don't have the time to use all sections of *ETE*?

If you do not have enough weeks or months to cover thoroughly all of the chapters, or enough class time to help your students work through all of *ETE*, there are several different approaches you can take. Read through the suggestions listed above and also consider doing one or more of the following:

1. Before your students begin their focus on reading biblical and theological materials in English, teach some of the academic vocabulary from the early chapters of *ETE* and also teach some of the reading and vocabulary strategies found in the Introduction and Chapter 1. This will help them with their other English reading assignments and it will also make for a more smooth transition once they begin *ETE*.
2. Use the Introduction and Chapters 1 and 2 for your students, because these give a broad foundation for all learners. Then use only the chapters that are the most important for their needs.
3. Use only the sections of each chapter, or selected chapters, that are most useful for your students' needs. For example, you might wish to use only the focused readings and theological vocabulary sections.
4. Make some sections of each chapter, or selected chapters, required for all students, and other sections optional.
5. Use some sections of each chapter, or selected chapters, for in-class work, and assign other sections for out-of-class work.
6. If your students speak the same native language, for each chapter assign different focused readings to small groups of students, who can then summarize the information for the others. While this procedure can be a shortcut for giving each class member a broad understanding of the content of the readings, we suggest that all students learn the theological vocabulary because these words are used widely in English theological publications.

What can you do if your students do not need everything in *ETE*?

If you have students with high advanced or superior English proficiency, or if you are teaching in a college, university, or seminary in a country where English is the medium of instruction, your students will probably need to use only selected parts of the *ETE* textbook.

1. We recommend that you follow the first four steps listed for students who are at a somewhat lower proficiency level than the target audience for *ETE* (pp. 13-14, *TG*). These steps will help you assess your students' English-language needs, level of motivation, use of effective reading and vocabulary learning strategies, and other factors that may affect their success in your class.

2. In determining which portions of *ETE* to use, note that in each chapter the different language skills and types of exercises are clearly marked. This makes it easy for you to select only the sections that are most essential for the needs of your students. You may want to omit some sections for your entire class, or you may want to individualize instruction by requiring some students to do sections that are optional for others (e.g., grammar activities).

What can you do if your students need to work on more skills and/or content areas than those addressed in *ETE*?

Your students may need to develop English skills not addressed in *ETE*, such as listening comprehension and note taking, making oral presentations, informal conversation, and writing. This can be a serious challenge, and if your students have very weak English skills, frequently there are no easy ways to solve this dilemma. Consider taking one or more of the following steps:

1. Plan for your students to have more time to study English—more months of English instruction and usually also more hours per week. The amount of time needed will depend upon several factors including their native language, their innate ability (language aptitude) and age, their current level of proficiency in each skill, the type and level of proficiency needed for each skill, the quality of English instruction they are receiving, the exposure they have to English outside of class, their motivation and their work habits. For learning materials, see the suggested materials and list of publishers in *ETE* Appendix 4, pp. 357-361 and *TG* Appendix 4, pp. 126-133.

2. Examine the procedures listed on pp. 13-16 (*TG*) for learners at a lower proficiency level. Implement as many of the steps as are appropriate for your learners.

3. Supplement your English instruction with learning activities that go beyond the classroom. For example, can you pair your students with native English speakers or non-native speakers who have a good command of English? If you are in an English-speaking environment, can you find host families or others who can help them with conversational English? Can you find relevant CD-ROM programs or audiotapes? Do your students have access to the Internet? If so, try to find practice exercises, podcasts, videos, and other materials that can supplement their learning. See *TG* Appendix 4, pp. 126-133.

Where can you find additional information to help you adapt *ETE* and teach it more successfully?

Most major publishers of ESL/EFL materials offer teacher preparation books for those who teach reading and vocabulary, and you can also find many good suggestions on the Internet. We have found two books to be particularly helpful for teachers who do not have a great deal of professional preparation in the field: *Essentials of Teaching Academic Reading* and *Essentials of Teaching Academic Vocabulary*. (See *TG* Appendix 5, pp. 134-142.) The first book focuses on the most basic and practical information you need in order to develop and teach an academic reading course. The second is written by Averil Coxhead, the compiler of the Academic Word List (AWL) used in *ETE*. It addresses key principles for teaching vocabulary and then discusses a wide variety of strategies and techniques for teaching and testing academic vocabulary. Each of these books provides a great deal of practical information for new and experienced ESL/EFL teachers and we believe they are especially valuable for those who need to make major changes in an existing curriculum, such as adapting materials or implementing new teaching procedures. For additional teacher preparation resources, see *TG* Appendix 5, pp. 134-142.

PART III: Preparing for Reading Theological Publications

To equip learners with the knowledge and skills they need in order to comprehend theological publications, *ETE* provides three main categories of learning experiences. While the majority of activities focus on the first two, developing reading skills and vocabulary skills, a smaller number address grammar skills. In this section of the *Teacher's Guide* we will discuss each of these types of learning experiences.

Reading Skills

As noted on p. xiii of the Preface to *ETE*, the primary goal of this textbook is to help non-native speakers of English develop and use the most important reading skills that good readers employ every day. The secondary goal is to introduce learners to important concepts and terminology used in theological writing. To meet these dual goals of acquiring the requisite language skills while also gaining a foundational grasp of theology, *ETE* provides five types of reading activities.

Reading Strategies

Better reading requires better reading strategies. To become more successful readers, nearly all ESL/EFL students need to learn and use more effective reading strategies. In addition to expanding their repertoire of strategies, learners need a great deal of practice in their use. The broad categories of reading strategies in *ETE* include planning, managing, evaluating, and expanding your learning (*ETE*, pp. 2-4); they also include reading at an appropriate pace, understanding what you read, and remembering what you read (*ETE*, pp. 20-22). Students practice applying these learning tools throughout the textbook. To locate where each individual strategy is explained and/or used, see the General Index in *ETE*, pp. 375-376. Because we believe that some reading strategies are especially important for reading success, we provide detailed information and practice on those strategies in the Reading for Meaning section of each chapter of the student textbook We encourage you to place special emphasis on these strategies throughout your teaching: locating the main idea, topic sentence, supporting details (pp. 33-35, 80-81, 114-117, 142-145, 173-174, 206-207, 236-237), skimming (pp. 35-37), scanning (pp. 81-82), using organizational markers (pp. 57-61, 207-212), outlining (p. 62), and SQ3R (pp. 272-274, 303).

Pre-Reading Exercises

Research shows that the more a reader knows about the subject matter of a paragraph or an entire reading, the easier it will be to understand the main ideas and the details (Seymour and Walsh 2006, 55). This is the reason that before every theological reading in the textbook we have included one or more pre-reading activities, which are usually exercises that allow students to practice one or more reading strategies. These include examining diagrams and charts, thinking about what you already know about a topic, skimming a reading to get the main ideas, scanning for specific words or terms, guessing what the main ideas are likely to be, circling terms that are new, and a number of other activities.

Readings

Each chapter has at least two short theological readings that address some aspect of the topic of that chapter, such as Humanity (Ch. 5) and Salvation and the Christian Life (Ch. 8). These readings not only provide introductory information about the topic, but they also offer multiple opportunities for students to apply the reading and vocabulary strategies they are learning. These readings have been simplified in two ways. First, the style of writing (sentence structure, vocabulary) is not as complex as that found in many theological publications. Second, for most readings, glosses (short definitions) are provided for the vocabulary items that learners are less likely to comprehend from the context. Many of the glosses are for low-frequency words—those words that should be at the bottom of the learners' list of priorities for vocabulary learning. Others are for more common vocabulary items employed in an unusual way in the reading passage. We suggest that you generally discourage your students from spending time to learn these definitions. Instead, remind them that we include the glosses to help them progress more quickly though the readings without having to consult a dictionary.

In addition to readings written especially for *ETE*, beginning with Chapter 8 we have included excerpts from theology textbooks, with no glosses provided. Each of the final three chapters has increasingly more material excerpted from theological publications. Chapter 10, for example, presents several pages from a lengthy article in a theological dictionary. We include these selections from published theological materials because we believe the earlier chapters of *ETE* have prepared your students to handle the complexities involved in theological writing. The next step for your learners will be to read a variety of theological publications written in English.

Post-Reading Exercises (Understanding the Reading)
To help learners understand and remember what they have read, every theological reading is followed by a section called Understanding the Reading, which has one or more exercises that facilitate reading comprehension. These include matching exercises, fill-in-the-blank exercises, charts to fill in, questions to answer about the reading, and group activities.

Review Exercises
The final section of each chapter includes review exercises that focus on understanding and applying the reading strategies of that chapter as well as reading comprehension questions related to one or more of the readings from the chapter. In addition, each chapter ends with a self-assessment, Evaluating Your Learning, which includes questions about the learners' use of effective reading strategies. This final exercise is intended to help learners not only keep their focus on important learning practices, but it should also encourage them to take more responsibility for monitoring their own progress and then take steps to improve their learning.

Vocabulary Skills
One of the most important assets belonging to good readers is a broad vocabulary that includes not only general everyday words but also a wide range of academic vocabulary. In addition, those who succeed in reading English theology materials must also know the most common theological terms and have the ability to learn as easily and quickly as possible the most important new vocabulary and terms they encounter in their readings.

Vocabulary Strategies
Your students can become more successful readers by expanding the number of vocabulary learning strategies that they use regularly. They may also need to discard some of their ineffective or less effective strategies. Beginning with the Introduction, every chapter focuses on identifying good strategies and/or applying these strategies to the learning of general vocabulary, general academic vocabulary, and theological vocabulary.

The Introduction to *ETE* presents some basic procedures your students should apply every time they read an academic publication—strategies for figuring out word meanings (pp. 5–6) and using a dictionary (p. 6). While it may take a great deal of practice for your learners to use these strategies consistently and successfully, after a few weeks or months they should be able to apply them more automatically. However, there are two key vocabulary learning procedures that should receive heavy emphasis throughout their study of *ETE:* using vocabulary cards (pp. 9-12), and using a vocabulary notebook (pp. 12-16).

One key vocabulary learning strategy, word analysis, receives special attention in five different chapters of *ETE*. When reading academic publications, learners need to know how to use all available clues to figure out the meanings of new words so that they don't have to look up those words in a dictionary. A useful tool is word analysis, which helps readers break down words into their individual parts. These word parts are the basic building blocks of many of our English words. Chapters 3 (pp. 91-96), 4 (pp. 126-129), 5 (pp. 153-157), 6 (pp. 182-186), and 8 (pp. 246-251) include sections that help learners identify prefixes, suffixes, and roots.

Academic Vocabulary

While they may know a large number of everyday vocabulary items, many ESL/EFL students lack an extensive vocabulary base for reading academic publications such as biblical and theological books and articles. To address this need, each of the ten chapters includes a section on general academic vocabulary. For each chapter, we have selected 20 or 24 words that meet two criteria: they occur in one or more of the reading passages of the current chapter, and they are from Averil Coxhead's Academic Word List (a widely used list of vocabulary that occur frequently in academic publications across a wide range of disciplines).

Many of the academic words chosen for *ETE* occur in more than one chapter, and some occur multiple times in nearly every chapter of the book. To help students learn selected AWL words, we include vocabulary exercises such as Fill in the Blank, Vocabulary in Context, Word Definitions, and Dictionary Use.

The Academic Word List (AWL) consists of 570 headwords, each from a different word family. A headword is the basic form of a word. For example, the headword *approach* includes *approachable, approached, approaches, approaching,* and *unapproachable* in the same word family. The 570 headwords of the AWL are grouped into ten sets, with the items in each successive set occurring less frequently than those in the preceding set. While most of these academic words are also used in newspapers, magazines, and other non-academic publications, they occur much more frequently in academic writing.[7]

ETE Appendix 2 (pp. 339-344), gives more information about the AWL and includes the 570 headwords. When you examine this list, you will see that not all of the AWL word families are represented in the *ETE* vocabulary exercises. If you have time, you may want to provide instruction for these additional word families. *ETE* Appendix 4 (pp. 357-361), suggests two books for teaching the AWL. In addition, there are Web sites with practice exercises such as http://www.academicvocabularyexercises.com/.[8]

To locate all of the AWL words in a reading or portion of a text, you can use the AWL Highlighter by Sandra Haywood (http://www.nottingham. ac.uk/~alzsh3/acvocab/awlhighlighter.htm).[9]

Theological Vocabulary

Coxhead's Academic Word List does not include words which are specific to a particular discipline, such as theology. However, each chapter of *ETE* includes the core theological vocabulary for the topic of that chapter. For example, Chapter 8 defines about three dozen terms related to salvation and the Christian life.

At the end of each theological vocabulary section, we have included one or more practice activities to help students remember the word definitions. In addition, in the Review section at the end of each chapter you will find a set of multiple-choice questions that deal with the theological vocabulary of that chapter, and they sometimes also review some of the vocabulary from previous chapters.

Grammar Skills

Theological writing often uses long, complex sentences that contain a number of clauses in a single sentence, thus making the subject matter even more difficult for readers to understand. While native English speakers sometimes have difficulty in comprehending the theological truths expressed in lengthy paragraphs made up of complex sentences, non-native English speakers may find the same paragraphs nearly impossible to read with adequate understanding. For this reason, *ETE* focuses on two types of clauses that are common in all academic publications, including theological writing: *adjective clauses* (sometimes called *adjectival clauses, relative clauses, dependent clauses,* or *subordinate clauses*) and *noun clauses.* Using a number of examples, each type of clause is explained in detail and a number of practice exercises are provided in the Grammar sections of Chapters 3, 4, 5, and 9 and an additional practice exercise may occur in the Review section of these chapters.

Teaching

Exploring Theological English

The purpose of this section is to help you teach *ETE* more effectively. Part I presents some general teaching suggestions for all chapters and some guidelines and principles for making your assessment more effective. Part II offers suggestions for teaching the various sections of each chapter. For additional suggestions for adapting the text to meet student needs, see *TG* Unit A, pp. 12-18. See also the *ETE* companion Web site, http://www.ExploringTheologicalEnglish.com.

PART I Suggestions for Getting Started

If this is your first time to teach *ETE*, we suggest that you not commit yourself to a set time frame for each chapter until you see how quickly your students can progress while continuing to have adequate comprehension. We have found that for most students the material is more challenging than either they or their teachers expect, and this results in taking longer for each chapter than originally anticipated.

General Guidelines for All Chapters
Listed below are some basic guidelines or suggestions that apply to the teaching of each chapter.

1. Make your lessons a positive learning experience so that students see reading as an enjoyable and important way to learn.
2. Model good reading and vocabulary learning strategies for your students. For example, talk about a word you looked up in a dictionary or the steps you used in guessing the meaning of a word in a book you are reading.
3. Have clear objectives for each part of your lesson. Remind your students frequently about why they are doing a particular activity or learning a new reading or vocabulary strategy.
4. Whenever possible, begin each lesson with a quick review of what your students learned in the previous lesson.
5. When introducing new topics, draw upon your students' background knowledge. Make connections to what they already know.

6. Use visuals (pictures, drawings, diagrams, charts) to help students understand new information.
7. Use a few key reading and/or vocabulary strategies repeatedly until students master them. Then continue to remind students of these strategies throughout the course.
8. Supplement each lesson with materials and activities that will challenge your more advanced students and additional materials and activities that are appropriate for learners who are having difficulty. Give individualized assignments as needed.
9. Review grammar and vocabulary by providing additional activities from English language textbooks. (See *TG* Appendix 4, pp. 126-133 for suggested teaching materials.)
10. When using small groups for discussions, vary the composition of the groups from time to time. For example, break students into equal-ability groups of three and then assign different discussion questions to each group according to their level of language ability. More difficult questions will go to those with a higher level of English ability and easier questions to those with a lower level of ability. At another time divide students into mixed-ability groups (or pairs) so that those with stronger language proficiency in English can help those who have weaker proficiency.
11. Make a range of Bible translations, dictionaries, and concordances available for use in your classroom.
12. Check the ETE companion Web site for additional resources and teaching suggestions (http://www.ExploringTheologicalEnglish.com).

Assessment

Appropriate learner assessment can make a very great difference in the overall effectiveness of learning—what your students learn, what activities and procedures they use, how quickly and how well they learn, and ultimately how effective they are in using their new language skills in their academic studies. However, to use this tool effectively requires following some basic principles of good assessment.

1. Planning for assessment should begin at the same time you plan your teaching of *ETE*, rather than after you begin teaching. When assessment is an afterthought tacked onto the end of the learning experiences, it is seldom as effective for the students.
2. Students need to understand the value of assessment for their overall learning. They need to "buy into" the idea that assessment is a helpful tool that will contribute to better learning and eventually to more productive academic study and future ministry.
3. Appropriate assessment affects students' rate of progress and keeps them progressing. If there is no assessment or if it occurs too infrequently, this lets the learners know that they can relax and

not work as hard, at least for a few days or weeks. This not only means that less learning occurs, but to achieve the level of language competence they need, these same students may need to spend additional weeks or months studying English.

4. Learning is nearly always more effective when learners are held accountable, but the accountability needs to be the right type—the kind that will motivate, encourage, point out directions to proceed, etc.

5. Before they begin the learning process, your students need to know what the assessment system will be like—what types of assessment will be used (show them samples) and the importance placed on formal assessment (e.g., a quiz or test) vs. informal assessment (e.g., a self-report or a checklist).

6. Assessment should reflect the goals and objectives of the learning program, the learning content, and the learning process. For example, if one of your goals is for learners to read more quickly without referring to a dictionary, you should have some means to assess their progress. If you teach basic theological terms related to salvation, you need to evaluate their knowledge of these terms.

7. Assessment strongly influences where students put their efforts and what they learn. The content and skills you choose to assess send a strong signal to your learners about what is important for them to learn. For example, if your students know they are going to be evaluated on their knowledge of theological vocabulary, they will make the learning of these terms a priority. On the other hand, if they know that you will never evaluate their learning of words from the Academic Word List, most of them will not make the effort to learn these words.

8. Study guides and review sheets are useful tools for helping students prepare for tests. They can include important terms and concepts, sample questions, and suggestions about how to prepare more effectively for a test.

9. Major decisions (e.g., whether a learner is ready for full-time study in English) should involve gathering various types of information (usually formal and informal) over a period of time. Major decisions should never be based on a single assessment of any kind.

10. Your assessment results provide valuable information you can use to adjust the content, learning procedures, and pace of your instruction.

PART II: Teaching Notes

Contents, Appendixes, Indexes

Contents
Although the *ETE* Contents (pp. vii–xi) precedes the Preface (pp. xiii–xvii), you may want to have your students read and discuss the Preface before you talk about the Contents.

1. **Introduction.** Highlight the importance of this section. The information your students learn in these pages will be used in every chapter of the book. Furthermore, the basic techniques or learning strategies will help your students become better readers who can read biblical and theological materials written in English.
2. **Chapters 1–10.** Use the Contents to help students understand the format of each chapter. Each of the ten chapters has many of the same major sections: Introduction, Vocabulary and Reading Skills, Focused Readings, Grammar and Vocabulary, Theological Vocabulary, and Review. Have your students look at these sections in at least one chapter. (The format of Chapter 3 is typical of many in the book.)
3. Identify the chapters or sections of chapters to which you will give special emphasis and/or identify sections you do not plan to use. For example, you may plan to give special attention to the Theological Vocabulary sections or you may plan not to assign the Grammar sections.

Appendixes

1. **Appendix 1** (pp. 335–337). Note that the first column of abbreviations are used in *ETE*. (Have students turn to p. 335.) You or your students may have books that use one of the other sets of abbreviations or a combination of two or more sets. You may also have books that use somewhat different abbreviations from those listed in this appendix.
2. **Appendix 2** (pp. 339–344). Tell your students that they will be learning many of these academic words as they study the *ETE* textbook. There is nothing that they need to do with these words at this time.
3. **Appendix 3** (pp. 345–356). This list of biblical and theological resources is primarily for your students to use after they have studied *ETE*.
4. **Appendix 4** (pp. 357–361). This list of ESL/EFL resources is primarily for your students to use after they have studied *ETE*.

Indexes

1.   Theology Index (pp. 367–373).
     a.   Examine the Theology Index, noting the type of information it contains.
     b.   Assign to each student a separate theological term (e.g., *exegesis, dynamic equivalent*) to look up in the Theology Index and then locate in the textbook.
     c.   Encourage students to use this index as needed.

2.   General Index (pp. 375–376).
     a.   Examine the General Index, noting the type of information it contains.
     b.   Assign to each student a separate vocabulary item (e.g., *collocations, synonym*) to look up in the General Index and then locate in the textbook.
     c.   Encourage students to use this index as needed.

Preface

The first paragraph of the Preface to the *ETE* student textbook (p. xiii) states the main goal for users of the book: to become more proficient at reading theological publications written in English. To meet this goal, students need to (1) acquire key reading skills (strategies, vocabulary, complex grammar) and (2) become familiar with important theological concepts and terminology. The Preface and Introduction to the student textbook deal largely with acquiring key reading skills. They should be given careful attention, making sure that students understand that this book is much more than an introduction to theology. Rather, students need to understand the importance of the sections dealing with reading, vocabulary, and grammar, and they need to remember that doing the exercises will help them read theology and other academic subjects more quickly and with better comprehension.

If your students are taking other English classes, either before or at the same time as they are studying *ETE*, consider using the Preface for a reading assignment. Whether it is used before your *ETE* class begins or on the first day of class, make certain that your students understand the goals of *ETE* and the other information from the Preface.

1.   Have students answer each of the questions on pp. xiii–xvi. To do this you may want to have them discuss their answers in small groups (either in their native language or in English), write short answers (either in their native language or in English), or demonstrate their understanding in another way.
2.   Be sure students understand the most important vocabulary used in the Preface. You may need to identify difficult words and talk about or pre-teach them before the students begin their reading.
3.   Use this opportunity to observe how easy or difficult it is for your students to read and comprehend the main ideas in the Preface.

How long does it take them to read these pages? For example, does it take them hours to read what you can read in a few minutes? Do they need to use their dictionaries excessively? What kinds of words are they looking up in their dictionaries? Can they differentiate between important words that convey the main idea and words that are of lesser importance? The answers to these questions will tell you a great deal about how your students approach the task of academic reading and about some of the reading and vocabulary learning skills you will need to emphasize in this course.

When discussing the Preface, you may want to use this time to let your students know about the requirements for your EBT class, including any ways that you plan to modify the use of the *ETE* textbook to accommodate their proficiency level in General Purpose English and/or their specific needs. For example, you may want to encourage your students to use their native language, rather than English, for answering questions that require longer, more complex answers. Or, you may require all students to have a particular kind of dictionary or notebook (see p. xvi).

If your students find reading the Preface to be especially difficult, this is a clear indication that the book is too advanced for their present level of English ability. You will then need to either postpone using the textbook until they have gained greater proficiency in General Purpose English as well as academic reading and vocabulary skills, or you will need to design a number of learning activities that will make the book easier to read and comprehend. (See *TG*, pp. 12–18 for information on teaching *ETE* to those whose English is at a lower proficiency level.)

Introduction

This is one of the most important chapters in the *ETE* textbook. Take adequate time to work through each section with your students, and plan to return frequently to this chapter as your class studies the remainder of the textbook.

Although the examples and exercises in the Introduction to *ETE* are related to biblical and theological studies, nearly all of the learning strategies are equally applicable to any type of academic reading. They are excellent strategies to introduce to your students in their English classes that precede their study of *ETE*.

Part I: Reading Strategies (*ETE*, pp. 1–4)

You may want to explain to your students that there are many types of learning strategies, but in this class you will focus only on those that are related to reading. Referring to the box on p. 1, point out that reading strategies constitute one broad category of learning strategies, and vocabulary strategies are a subcategory of reading strategies. Part 1 (pp. 1–4) focuses on strategies that are related to the reading process while Part 2 (pp. 5–17) deals specifically with strategies for learning new vocabulary words. As you discuss these two types with your students, you may find that it is easier to talk about reading and vocabulary strategies at the same time, rather than trying to keep the two separate.

Discuss the reading strategies on pp. 1-4 with your students. Which ones have they been using and which new to them? Which are easy to do and which are difficult? Can you add other strategies to this list? Does anyone in your class use another reading strategy that he or she believes is effective?

This chapter lists strategies that are common to good readers. However, many students use strategies that are ineffective and often detrimental to good reading skills. With the help of your class, make a list of less effective strategies (e.g., translating everything into the native language, memorizing the dictionary meaning of every new word). Then discuss steps they can take to apply more effective strategies while avoiding or minimizing the use of the less effective ones.

You may want to make a poster of reading strategies and another of vocabulary strategies. These can be displayed in the classroom so that you can refer to them frequently. It will also serve as a reminder to the students that these learning strategies are important tools for helping them become better readers.

We suggest that you have each student choose one strategy for special focus in the early lessons of *ETE*, or you may prefer to have them choose a new strategy each week or every two weeks. Make a chart that lists each student and his or her special focus strategies. Keep the list nearby so that you can remind each one of (1) the purpose of his or her strategy (i.e., the benefits in terms of better reading skills), (2) the need to continue applying the strategy, (3) any special tips on how to implement the strategy, and (4) his or her progress in using the strategy.

Part II: Vocabulary Strategies (*ETE*, pp. 5–17)

Learning New Vocabulary (pp. 5–8)

Figuring Out Word Meanings. In this section students are introduced to three strategies and given a little practice with each strategy. Remind them that in every chapter of the textbook they will get more practice on each strategy. With continued focus, these strategies should become more automatic.

Using a Dictionary. The better your learners are at applying these two important strategies, the more successful they will be as readers. We suggest that you first check to see how effective your learners are in dictionary use and then discuss and demonstrate each step of these strategies. With frequent reminders over a few weeks, your students should be able to apply these strategies fairly automatically. (Ch. 2, pp. 63-67, discusses different types of dictionaries with special emphasis on theological dictionaries.)

Linking Unfamiliar Words to Familiar Words and Phrases. Knowing common collocations (two or more words that often combine in a phrase) is important for reading more quickly and with better comprehension. However, this skill is even more important for writing well. If your class also emphasizes writing in English, you may wish to make available to your students a copy of *Oxford Collocations Dictionary for Students of English.* (See *TG* Appendix 4: ESL/EFL Student Resources, p. 133.)

Organizing New Vocabulary for Future Learning (pp. 9–16)
Using Vocabulary Cards. The most important objective for both vocabulary cards (also called flash cards) and the vocabulary notebook is for students to learn key vocabulary items so that they will no longer need to use a dictionary to look up these words when they encounter them again in their reading. However, many students lose sight of this objective and instead think only about fulfilling the requirement of making the required number of cards or entering the required number of items into their notebooks. As their instructor, you will need to remind them frequently that these are merely steps to help them achieve the greater objective of being able to read academic writing more quickly and with greater comprehension, without having to stop frequently to look up another vocabulary word.

Perhaps most of your students have been using vocabulary cards since they began to learn English. They may have found good ways to enter information on the cards, organize the cards, and use them to learn new words. However, many students will need help in order to devise a system that works well for serious academic work such as the study of theology. Nearly all students will profit from the type of assessment that encourages them to learn the information on their cards, and thus no longer need to continue looking up the same words in a dictionary.

1. Elicit information from your class about their current use of vocabulary cards and then contrast their approach with the advantages and disadvantages of the system introduced in this section.
2. Provide your students with three to five completed vocabulary cards for the Introduction and first two or three chapters (or sections of chapters) and require them to make a minimum number of additional cards (e.g., ten). If your students have the tendency to make far more cards than they can use, you may also want to suggest a maximum number of cards per lesson or per week.
3. Encourage students who have computers to make their vocabulary cards on their computers.
4. As your students begin using this system, check to see that they are making cards for only the most important words and that they are writing useful and appropriate information on each card.
5. Every few days, ask the class about their use of the vocabulary cards. Where and when do they use their cards? How frequently do they review their cards?
6. On a regular basis require students to turn in cards for you to check.

7.   On a regular basis evaluate your students' command of key vocabulary.

Using a Vocabulary Notebook. Some students may prefer to use only vocabulary cards and not make a vocabulary notebook. However, most will find that cards are more useful for some words or phrases and that the notebook is more useful for others.

For many students, the following are the most challenging aspects of keeping a vocabulary notebook:

- Finding a system that separates words into appropriate categories, allows for the easy addition of more words, is convenient to use, and is not overly complex.
- Selecting important words and phrases for the notebook, rather than entering every new word or phrase. Many students will need help in identifying the significant words and phrases.
- Using the notebook on a regular basis.

The student text suggests a number of ways to handle a vocabulary notebook. Each student will have to develop a system that works best for his or her needs. Most will have at least one or two false starts before finding the most optimal system for their personal use.

1.   Help your students set up the categories for their notebooks. If your class has not used vocabulary notebooks in previous studies, you will probably need to work with the entire class to devise a system that will work well for their needs.
2.   Show samples from previous classes and also encourage learners to share their ideas for effective ways to organize their notebooks.
3.   Help students differentiate between more important words and phrases and those that are less important. If your students insist on including all new words (those that are important and those that are of lesser importance), suggest that they have another section in their notebooks for the less important words. By doing this, it will be easier for them to focus on the more important items and yet not totally abandon learning those that are of lesser significance at this point in their academic reading.
4.   Encourage students who have computers to devise a computer-based system for organizing their vocabulary notebooks. However, they should still keep notebooks for writing down new items in class and in individual study.
5.   Every few days ask your students about their progress in adding items to their vocabulary notebooks.
6.   On a regular basis require your students to show you their vocabulary notebooks so that you can check their entries and their overall organization. This step has several benefits: it encourages students to keep a vocabulary notebook, it helps you to know how successfully they can use this vocabulary learning system, it shows you the types of words they find challenging, and it helps you know

how to adjust your teaching to meet the needs of each student and the class as a whole.

7. On a regular basis evaluate your students' knowledge of the most important vocabulary items that are likely to occur throughout the book and in other theological writing. By testing only the most important vocabulary items, your students will automatically place more emphasis on learning these words and less emphasis on the others.

Getting Started

Some teachers and students do well with learning contracts. For this chapter you could ask your students to list on paper three steps that they plan to take in order to become better readers. Have each student sign two copies of his or her contract, one to keep and one to give to you. Once every few days or weeks ask the students to report on how well they are meeting the steps listed in their contracts.

Chapter 1: Starting with the Bible

Some of the teaching notes for Chapter 1 apply only to this chapter. Others are equally applicable to the following chapters, even though they are not repeated for each chapter. We suggest that you study carefully the notes for Chapter 1 and return to them as needed.

The first paragraph of the Preface to the *ETE* student textbook (p. xiii) states the main goal for users of the book: to become more proficient at reading theological publications written in English. To meet this goal, students need to (1) acquire key reading skills (strategies, vocabulary, complex grammar) and (2) become familiar with important theological concepts and terminology. While the Preface and Introduction to the student textbook deal largely with the first goal, Chapters 1–10 give major emphasis to the second goal while continuing to address the first goal. In particular, Chapters 1 and 2 should be given very careful attention because they provide a broad framework for biblical and theological studies. This framework gives students a foundation for understanding the theological discussions in later chapters as well as comprehending other biblical and theological writings. In addition, Chapter 1 helps students to become more competent readers by introducing new learning strategies.

Opening Bible Verses and Introduction (p. 19)

Each chapter in the student text begins with three short sections: one or more Bible verses, a short description of the chapter content, and a chapter introduction. The opening verses and the Introduction (usually no more than a few short paragraphs) relate to the biblical or theological theme of the chapter.

For students who are at a lower proficiency level in General Purpose English, first have them read in their native-language Bibles the opening verses and the relevant Bible passage for the Introduction (e.g., Neh 8 for

Ch. 1). Then have them read the verses and Introduction in English. If you discuss these sections with your class, you may want to do this in their native language.

Part I: Reading Strategies (pp. 20–22)

In academic settings, reading is the primary means for learning new information and gaining access to alternative explanations and interpretations. Reading provides the foundation for synthesis and critical evaluation skills. Reading is also the primary means for independent learning, whether the goal is improving performance in academic tasks, improving language skills, or learning more about specific subject matter such as theology.

Developing more effective reading habits is critical to your students' success in becoming more competent readers. By utilizing the three categories of strategies introduced in Chapter 1 (reading at an appropriate pace, understanding what you read, and remembering what you read), your students will not only be more successful in reading and understanding the content of *ETE*, but they will also leave this course with valuable skills that will help them comprehend all types of academic and nonacademic writing. For this reason, you should return to these reading strategies frequently, reminding your students to apply the strategies in their independent reading as well as in their classroom activities.

This section introduces a total of 19 strategies. Your primary goal for now is to help your students understand the value of effective reading strategies and to identify some strategies they already use. At this point you should not ask them to attempt to apply these new strategies to their reading. That will come later as they work through the student textbook.

1. Prepare a short questionnaire (in English or the students' native language), in which you ask about your students' current reading habits. To get a general idea about their use of some or all of the 19 strategies, you could use questions like those in Group 1; for more detailed information, you could use questions like those in Group 2.

Group 1:

Sample Questions	Yes	Sometimes	No
a. Do you always read at the same pace?			
b. Do you look over a paragraph or section before reading it carefully?			
c. When reading new information, do you try to determine the main ideas that you need to remember?			
d. When reading new information, do you stop to think about what you already know about the subject?			

Group 2:

a. Do you always read at the same pace? If not, when do you read more quickly? When do you read more slowly?

b. Do you look over a paragraph or section before reading it carefully? If so, what do you do?

c. When reading new information, do you try to determine the main ideas that you need to remember, or do you try to remember everything the paragraph says? Describe what you often do.

d. When reading new information, do you stop to think about what you already know about the subject? Describe what you often do.

In order not to overwhelm your students, include on your questionnaire only the strategies that you think are most important for your class to focus on at this time.

For classes at a lower English proficiency level, you may want to ask only four or five questions. For these students, the section on reading at an appropriate pace is probably less applicable because they may not be able to read more quickly. Likewise, thinking ahead to what may be said next may not be possible. However, strategies such as finding the main idea, scanning for key terms, recognizing organizational markers, and underlining or highlighting are very important for learners at all levels.

2. Tabulate the answers to your reading strategies questionnaire, and then discuss the results with your class.
   a. Comment on their answers to each question. For example, if students say that they always read at the same pace, ask them about the advantages and disadvantages of this practice.
   b. For each question, have the class read the corresponding sections on pp. 20–22. For example, for the first question listed above, have them read the section on p. 20, Reading at an Appropriate Pace. Then discuss the reasons for varying the pace of their reading.

3. Choose one or two strategies for the entire class to focus on as they begin Chapter 1, or for more advanced classes you may want to have each individual focus on one or two of the most important strategies for his or her reading success. As the students gain control over the selected strategies, have them add more strategies for special attention.

4. You may wish to make a poster that lists the strategies your class has chosen as most important. Display this poster (or list) so that students will be reminded every day to apply the strategies.

5. As you continue to use the *ETE* textbook, ask your students about their use of these reading strategies from Chapter 1. Remind them of the benefits of acquiring and using effective strategies, and

comment on their progress in developing good reading habits. Also remind them of the fact that reading in English will become much more enjoyable once they experience the breakthrough that comes from moving beyond the laborious process of stopping to look up every new vocabulary item and instead apply the strategies that will help them understand and remember what they have read.

Part II: Focused Reading (pp. 22–29)

Each of the ten chapters has one or more sections called Focused Reading. These sections introduce students to theological content of the chapter and provide opportunities for them to practice their reading and vocabulary learning strategies. They generally include three subsections: questions or activities that precede the reading, the reading, and questions or activities based on the content of the reading.

The Bible and Related Studies (pp. 22–29)

Pre-Reading. Pre-reading activities are designed to help students begin to think about the topic of the reading, thus making it easier for them to read more efficiently and comprehend more fully. These activities often include items that require the readers to do one or more of the following:

- think about and organize what they already know about the topic
- examine the reading to get a general idea about the content (e.g., look at the heading, subheadings, information that is in bold or italics)
- determine the main points
- locate specific information such as important terms
- examine charts, diagrams, and pictures, and comment on their relationship to one or more of the main points
- predict one or more of the most important subtopics in the reading
- write questions that they believe will be answered in the reading

1. You may need to help your students examine Figure 1.1 on p. 24. Ask questions about the diagram, such as the following:
   a. What are the two main sections of the biblical text?
   b. What are four types of theology?
   c. (for more advanced students) What do you think "Going There" means? "Coming Back Again"? The purpose of asking questions such as these is not to find the correct answer at this time, but rather to help students focus on the questions that they should be able to answer after doing the reading.
2. Discuss their answers to the Pre-Reading questions 1-3 on p. 22. For question 2, encourage students to guess at the meaning of one of the terms they selected.

3.　With the help of your class, list the reading strategies from pp. 20-22 that are used in the Pre-Reading activities on p. 22. Their answers should include the following strategies, and they may also list others.

　　a.　Study the diagrams, charts, and pictures (#9, p. 21).
　　b.　Scan for key terms (#8, p. 21).
　　c.　Underline or highlight the new terms and important points (#1, p. 22).

Reading

1.　Point out the organization of this reading passage, which is similar to others in the text.

　　a.　The directions are the same for all readings.
　　b.　Each reading has a title (e.g., The Bible and Related Studies, p. 22).
　　c.　The reading is divided into sections, each with a title (e.g., Studying and Applying the Biblical Text: "Going There and Coming Back Again," p. 23, and "Going There," p. 25). These are divided into subsections (e.g., Language, p. 25), which are divided into still smaller sections.
　　d.　Paragraph markers used in the readings allow for easy reference.
　　e.　Key terms are often in bold.

2.　Go over the directions carefully, expanding on each of the items.

　　a.　Definitions. Point out that the glosses at the right margin provide short definitions for some of the difficult vocabulary. For example, the gloss *obvious, clear* goes with the word *apparent* in paragraph 1, line 2, and the gloss *interested in* goes with *fascinated by* in line 4 of the same paragraph. Most of the glossed words are general purpose or academic vocabulary; very few are theological vocabulary. The purpose of these glosses is to help readers understand the text without having to stop to look up unfamiliar vocabulary.

　　　　Some of the glossed words may be items for which your students will want to make vocabulary cards or make an entry in their vocabulary notebooks. We suggest, however, that learners use cards or notebooks for very few of the general purpose and academic words, and instead reserve their use for key theological terms. Otherwise, they are likely to select far too many words for their vocabulary cards or vocabulary notebooks, rather than only the most important words they need to learn.

　　b.　Dictionary use. Encourage students not to look up every unfamiliar word in a dictionary. There are at least three steps you can take to help them avoid this practice. If your students are at a lower proficiency level in English, you will probably need to take all three of these steps:

- Review with your class the most important vocabulary learning strategies on pp. 5-7 of the student text.
- Add more glosses for your students.
- Teach key vocabulary before your learners do the reading. For examples of exercises you can construct, see the Pre-Reading matching exercises in Chapter 9 (p. 274). Also see the Fill in the Blank and Vocabulary in Context exercises in Chapter 1 (pp. 31-32). The matching exercises are generally easier to construct than the other two types, but each type can help your students to learn new vocabulary in context.

   c.   Underlining. Students should use underlining (or highlighting) to mark the most important material so that they can review more easily. Because learners often want to underline or highlight too much material, you will probably need to help your students know what to mark. Seymour and Walsh (2006, 73-74) suggest that learners underline or highlight no more than 10% of the text, reserving this for important definitions, concepts, and summary sentences. They also suggest that learners refrain from underlining or highlighting the first time they read a passage.

   d.   Comments and questions. For the first few readings, you will probably need to help your learners discover the types of comments and questions that will be helpful as they review the reading passage. Consider allowing your learners to write comments and questions in their native language.

3.   Encourage students to apply one new reading or vocabulary strategy as they read this first passage. You may want to have all students focus on the same strategy for the first lesson or two.

4.   Because this is a long reading, you may want to divide it into two or three major sections, treating each section as a separate reading. For example, ask pre-reading questions only for the first section, and after students have read that section, they should answer questions to demonstrate their understanding of the content. Then, follow the same procedures for the next major section of the reading.

5.   Work through the reading (or major section) in class, using the following procedures:

   a.   Pre-teach any vocabulary that you know will be challenging for your students. For lower-level students, you may need to do this for each paragraph as you move through the reading, rather than doing it only once for the entire reading or major section.

   b.   Have students read silently one longer paragraph or two or three short paragraphs.

   c.   Discuss the main points and answer questions.

    d.   Check to see that they are underlining (or highlighting) main points and important terms.

    e.   Ask about the comments and questions they have written in the margin.

6.   Make sure your students understand the importance of each of the six areas of study (e.g., language) and also know the important terms for each area (e.g., textual criticism). Whenever possible, illustrate the areas with examples such as the following:

    a.   Translation. Show two or more English translations. If you have more than one translation in the students' native language, show these as well.

    b.   Literary Form (Genre). Point out books, chapters, or verses of the Bible that are written in poetry and those that are narrative in style. If possible, do this for English and their native language.

    c.   Theology. Show a variety of theology books (historical, biblical, systematic, practical).

Understanding the Reading. Understanding the Reading sections include a number of questions that focus on the biblical and theological content of the reading. For some readings, you may need to construct additional exercises to help your students learn the material.

Occasionally, students are asked to write a short answer (e.g., pp. 28–29, # 2–3). For questions like these you may want your students to use their native language for writing their answers.

Part III: Vocabulary and Reading Skills (pp. 30–37)

In addition to general academic vocabulary, the Vocabulary and Reading Skills section of each chapter usually provides additional practice on theological vocabulary as well as more detailed explanations of important reading strategies and practice in applying those strategies.

If you think your students will find this Chapter 1 vocabulary to be particularly challenging, you may want to do Part III before Part II.

General Academic Vocabulary (pp. 30–32)

Before you teach Chapter 1, we suggest that you first learn more about Averil Coxhead's Academic Word List (AWL) which is used throughout *ETE* as the source for all words in the academic vocabulary sections. Appendix 2 in the student text gives an overview of the AWL and lists the headword for each of the 570 word families as well as the most frequently occurring word for each family. You can also use this appendix as a quick reference to see all of the AWL words found in *ETE* practice exercises and the chapter in which each word appears. To learn even more about the AWL, go to the Web sites listed in Appendix 2 of the student text (p. 339). You may also want to purchase a copy of Coxhead's book, *Essentials of Teaching Academic Vocabulary* (see *TG* Appendix 5, pp. 134–142).

Because most of the academic vocabulary in this chapter will be familiar to your students, they will probably mark most words in the first exercise, Chapter 1 Vocabulary, with a 1 and may mark a few words with a 2. If they mark a large number of these words with a 2 or 3, this is an indication that the Chapter 1 reading passages are likely to be too difficult and that you will need to provide additional glosses for the readings or construct exercises to pre-teach vocabulary before they continue with the readings. Also, if the Chapter 1 academic vocabulary is particularly challenging for your class, this means that the vocabulary in the following chapters will quickly become far too difficult for them.

1.   As your students work through the exercises, remind them to pay particular attention to the words they marked with a 2 or 3.
2.   For the Vocabulary in Context exercise, point out that by using a dictionary students do not always come up with the correct meaning of a word as it is used in a particular context. You may need to work through two or three items with the class so that they will understand how to choose the correct definition for the context.
3.   After completing these exercises, have students return to the Chapter 1 Vocabulary list (p. 30) and mark the words again with 1, 2, or 3.
4.   For particularly difficult vocabulary, your students may want to make vocabulary cards or set up a general academic vocabulary section in their vocabulary notebooks.
5.   For lower-level students, you may need to construct additional exercises.

Theological Vocabulary (p. 33)
Word Families in Context. This short section appears in nearly every chapter. For most students the exercises will be quite easy, so you may want to assign it as homework.

Reading for Meaning (pp. 33–37)
Each of the Reading for Meaning sections expands on strategies from the Introduction (pp. 20-22) and includes practice exercises for using selected strategies. Strategies that require a great deal of practice (e.g., locating the main idea) occur in more than one chapter.

The Chapter 1 strategies, *Locating the Main Idea and Topic Sentence* and *Skimming for the Main Ideas in the Reading*, are two of the most important strategies your students need to develop in order to become more proficient readers. Therefore, your goal should be for all students to become highly competent at using these two strategies.

Reading Strategy: Locating the Main Idea and Topic Sentence. You will probably need to work through this section very carefully with your students because locating the main idea can be very challenging initially, and locating the topic sentence can be even more challenging. It is especially important that they become good at finding the main idea, as this will allow them to more fully understand what they read and it will also allow them to take more relevant notes.

1. Locating the main idea. You may need to find additional paragraphs for your students to use in locating the main idea. To make the task easier, give your students two or three choices from which to select the main idea. This strategy also occurs in Chapter 3 (pp. 80-81), Chapter 4 (pp. 114-117), Chapter 5 (pp. 142-145), Chapter 6 (pp. 173-175), Chapter 7 (pp. 206-207), and Chapter 8 (pp. 236-237).
2. Locating the topic sentence. You may need to find additional paragraphs for your students to use in locating the topic sentence. In selecting paragraphs, make sure that each one has a very clear topic sentence. This strategy also occurs in Chapter 3 (pp. 80-81), Chapter 4 (pp. 114-117), Chapter 5 (pp. 142-145), Chapter 6 (pp. 173-175) and Chapter 7 (pp. 206-207).

Reading Strategy: Skimming for the Main Ideas in the Reading. In most classes of ESL/EFL learners, very few have used skimming as one of their reading strategies. Some students may even object to doing this, saying that they need to know every detail, and the only way for them to do this is to read each word of each sentence very carefully and slowly.

1. You may need to convince your students that skimming is a strategy that they can learn to do well and that it will be very beneficial in helping them read more quickly and understand more completely what they are reading. See pp. 35-36 and also p. 21 for more information on the purpose for skimming.
2. Check to make sure that each student knows the steps in skimming (p. 36) and has ample practice in applying these steps.
3. If this is particularly difficult for your students, or if they say that it is not useful, assure them that with more practice it will become easier and they will also come to see the benefits of learning to skim a reading passage before reading it more carefully.

Part IV: Focused Reading (pp. 37–44)

Carefully work through this reading before assigning it to your students. If you think the vocabulary will be too challenging for them, pre-teach the more difficult words.

The Worldview of Biblical Writers (pp. 37–39)

Pre-Reading. Be sure your students complete this activity. Discuss the answers before beginning the reading. You may also want to give an oral summary of the reading in the students' native language and/or have them read a summary written in their language.

Reading. Unless your students are at a very high level, we suggest that you work through the reading in class, stopping to discuss each paragraph or main point. Check to see that they are following the directions for using the glosses, underlining, and writing comments or questions in the margin.

Understanding the Reading. Note that on p. 39, students are directed to review the steps for making vocabulary cards and then they are to make cards for five to ten words. For additional instructions, see *TG*, pp. 30-31.

Translation Philosophies of the Bible (pp. 40–44)
This section will be more interesting if you can bring to class a number of different translations of the Bible. Ideally, you will have translations in the students' native languages as well as a number of English translations.

Pre-Reading

1. Be sure your students complete the Pre-Reading activities. Discuss the answers to these questions and remind them of the benefits of learning to skim a reading.

2. With your class, examine Figure 1.2 on p. 43. As appropriate, ask questions such as the following:
    a. Which versions do you own or have available to use?
    b. Which versions do you find easier to read and understand?
    c. Which versions do you use for serious Bible study or for use in class?
    d. Which versions do you have for your native language? How do you use each one?

3. If your students have access to the Internet, have them go to the Bible Gateway site (http://www.biblegateway.com). This site contains more than a hundred online searchable Bibles in English and 50 other languages.
    a. Have your students look up the same verse in three or more versions of the Bible. Then write out the verse and include the Bible versions used (e.g., John 3:16 in the King James Version, the New International Version, and the New Living Translation).
    b. If this site has more than one Bible version for your students' native language, have them look up verses in two or more versions.

Reading. If you think this section will be too difficult, follow the suggestions for the preceding reading.

Understanding the Reading

1. Discuss different translation philosophies by showing parallel passages in several English translations.

2. You may want students to translate passages from their native language into English in order to discuss and reinforce different philosophies of Bible translation. This can be especially useful when they have two or more very different translations in their native language.

Part V: Review (pp. 44–48)

Each chapter of *ETE* ends with one or more review exercises that focus on the major sections in the chapter. This is followed by a final exercise, Evaluating Your Learning, that requires students to recall their use of a number of reading and vocabulary strategies.

There are a number of ways you can use these review exercises. For example, you may have students do the exercises individually, in pairs, or in small groups; you may want to use one or more sections of the Review as a chapter test; or you may assign some of the exercises as homework. However, we suggest that at the end of each chapter you discuss the Evaluating Your Learning exercise with your students. This is a good opportunity to remind them of the importance of the learning strategies listed and to answer questions about strategy use.

After completing Chapter 1, you may want to do the following:

1. Check vocabulary notebooks and cards. Collect class words and prepare a master list to review with your class.
2. Select a paragraph from the following chapter for students to find the main idea and topic sentence.
3. Select a reading passage from the following chapter for students to demonstrate their skimming skills.
4. Ask students to write in their journal about their learning. You may want to use questions such as these: Which English translation do you prefer to use? What is one new thing that you have learned about the English Bible? (Students with a lower proficiency level in English may need to write their answers in their native language.)

Chapter 2: Introducing Theology

As noted in the *TG* at the beginning of Chapter 1 (*TG*, p. 32), the first two chapters provide a broad framework for studying the theological concepts presented in later chapters of the text. For this reason, Chapters 1 and 2 should be given careful attention.

Many of the teaching notes for Chapter 1 (*TG*, pp. 32–42) are equally applicable for Chapter 2 and all following chapters. You may want to review those notes before starting to teach this new chapter.

As you begin Chapter 2, you should have a much better idea about your students' level of English proficiency as well as their ability to do the readings and complete the exercises. If they found Chapter 1 to be especially difficult, you should be prepared to adjust your teaching procedures for Chapter 2. (See *TG*, pp. 12–16.)

Part I: Focused Reading (pp. 50–54)

What is Theology? (pp. 50–51)
Pre-Reading. Do the Pre-Reading question as an in-class activity.

1. Write on the board the question, What is theology?
2. Have students write preliminary definitions in their books (in their native language or in English).
3. Discuss their answers. Remind students that after studying this chapter they will have more complete answers to this question.

Reading. Follow the procedures used for Chapter 1, making adjustments as needed.

Understanding the Reading. Depending on the needs of your class, you may wish to do some or all of the following:

1. Encourage students to write their definitions in their own words, rather than copying word for word from the text.
2. Have students answer the questions individually and then discuss the answers with the class.
3. Allow students to work in small groups or pairs. Then each group or pair reports to the class on their definitions.
4. Write some of the definitions on the board. This may help the students who need to see the definitions as well as hear them.

Types of Theology (pp. 52–54)
For classes with a higher level of English proficiency, consider making this reading an out-of-class assignment. For use as an in-class reading, follow the procedures used in Chapter 1, making adjustments as needed.

Part II: Vocabulary and Reading Skills (pp. 54–62)

General Academic Vocabulary (pp. 54–56)
Word Definitions (p. 56) is a new type of exercise. Before assigning this exercise, check the definitions for these items in the English-only dictionaries your students use. If they have more than one dictionary available, check to see which one is most appropriate to use for this exercise. For classes that include learners at different levels, you may want to require more advanced students to use a different dictionary from the one used by those with a lower level of English proficiency. Work through the example with the class, and help them with the first item or two if necessary.

Reading for Meaning (pp. 57–62)
Reading Strategy: Using Organizational Markers

1. Make sure your students understand the purpose of organizational markers (p. 57).
2. Focus on one type of organizational marker at a time (e.g., markers for examples and illustrations, pp. 57-58).
3. Discuss the specific markers and examples on the chart (p. 58).
4. Assist students as needed in completing the exercises (p. 58).
5. Repeat this process for each category of markers.

These three types of organizational markers are used many times throughout *ETE*. If your students find them difficult, or if they are not making good use of these markers to help them understand what they are reading, you may need to provide more exercises and/or give frequent reminders to look for markers in their *ETE* readings. In addition, you can find supplementary exercises on the Internet. Use a search engine such as Google to search for *organizational markers* or *organizational structure* and the specific type of marker, such as *examples and illustrations* or *illustrations*.

Chapter 7 (pp. 207-212) introduces two additional types of organizational markers: comparison and contrast, and cause and effect.

Reading Strategy: Outlining. This strategy is explained in Chapter 2 (p. 62), and in some of the following chapters learners are asked to make outlines. However, because of its importance in helping readers understand complex reading passages, you may want to require your students to make an outline of at least one reading, or part of a reading, in every chapter.

1. Write the outline (p. 62) on the board or on an overhead transparency, and then enter new information as appropriate.
2. Have students read the steps for outlining (p. 62).
3. Have students read paragraph 2 (p. 52) on historical theology. Go over the main idea, sub-points, and specific values provided in the outline (p. 62).
4. Have students read paragraph 3 (pp. 52-53).
5. Ask students for the main idea, and have them write it on their outline.
6. Guide students through the sub-points and specific values for biblical theology as they fill in their outlines.
7. Have students complete parts III and IV in pairs or on their own.
8. Check the answers.

Part III: Using Theological Dictionaries (pp. 63–67)

Types of Dictionaries (pp. 63–64)

1. Provide as many examples as you can of each of the four types of dictionaries: English-only, bilingual, ESL/EFL learner's, and theological. Ask students to bring their dictionaries to class.
2. Discuss the four types of dictionaries.
   a. Point out the distinctive features, preferred uses, and strengths and weaknesses of each type.
   b. Ask students to describe what they like or don't like about specific dictionaries.

If your students are not familiar with the features of an English-only dictionary or an ESL/EFL learner's dictionary, consider using some learning activities to promote more effective dictionary use. Most ESL/EFL learner's dictionaries provide a separate workbook or CD-ROM with learning activities. Some also have a section of exercises in the dictionary. For some of the more popular ESL/EFL dictionaries, the publisher has a companion Web site with learning activities. See *ETE* Appendix 4 (pp. 357-361) for recommended dictionaries.

Special Features of Theological Dictionaries (pp. 65–67)

1. Discuss each of the special features (pp. 65-66) with your class. Have them find examples of each feature (e.g., entry word, word in original language). If each class member has a copy of the same theological dictionary, have the entire class (or small groups) look up the same set of words and then report on their findings. For example, they could look up *Abba* to find the definition, the biblical references, and the cross-references.
2. Assign the exercises on pp. 66-67 and have students compare their answers with a partner.
3. You may want to have each student examine a different theological dictionary and report on the special features.

For additional learning activities related to using a theological dictionary, see Cheri Pierson's *Dictionary of Theological Terms in Simplified English: Student Workbook* (2003), pp. 10-22.

Part IV: Focused Reading (pp. 68–72)

By now you should have a good idea about your students' strengths and weaknesses as readers, and you probably have some ideas about how to change your teaching procedures to better meet student needs. The following questions may help you focus more specifically on the types of changes you need to make:

1. Am I giving my students enough (too much) help with any aspect of the reading process?

2.   Are my students applying the strategies and skills they already know, or are they depending on me (or other students) too much?
3.   Am I moving too quickly (or too slowly) through the readings?
4.   Am I making enough use of the students' native languages (or too much use)?
5.   Do I need to make more individual assignments in order to challenge the stronger students and/or assist the weaker students?
6.   Do I need to prepare study guides to help my students prepare for tests?
7.   Am I using quizzes and tests to help students learn theological content and also effective reading and vocabulary skills?
8.   Am I modifying my teaching based on the results of the quizzes, tests, and other student feedback?

Intellectual Issues that Affect Theological Viewpoinrt (pp. 68-72)
Review the procedures you used for earlier Focused Readings, and modify them as needed.

Part V: Review (pp. 72–76)
Review the procedures you used in Chapter 1 (*TG*, p. 42), and modify them as needed.

Chapter 3: God
Many of the teaching notes for Chapter 1 (*TG*, pp. 32-42) are equally applicable for Chapter 3. You may want to review those notes before starting to teach this new chapter.

Part I: Vocabulary and Reading Skills (pp. 77–82)

General Academic Vocabulary (pp. 77–79)
This section includes two new types of exercises. Word Selection (p. 78) is similar to Word Families in Context, which appears in Chapters 1 and 2 (pp. 33, 57) and Dictionary Use (p. 79) is similar to Word Definitions in Chapter 2 (p. 56). Word Selection should be easy for your students, but they may need some help with Dictionary Use. Before assigning this exercise, check the definitions for these items in the English dictionaries your students use. If they have more than one dictionary available, check to see which one is most appropriate to use for this exercise. For classes that include learners at different levels, you may want to require students to use the dictionary that is most appropriate for each person's level of English proficiency.

Reading for Meaning (pp. 80–82)
Reading Strategy: Locating the Main Idea and Topic Sentence. Although your students were introduced to this strategy in Chapter 1 (pp. 33–35), they will need much more practice in order to identify the main idea and topic sentence. You may want to select additional paragraphs from *ETE*

(or other publications) to provide extra practice. In addition, they will encounter the strategy again in Chapters 4-8.

Reading Strategy: Scanning for Specific Information

1. Review the steps for scanning (p. 81) with your students.
2. Answer the first question (p. 82) as a class activity together.
3. Have students work individually to answer the second question. (p. 82).
4. If your students need more practice with scanning, use the Theological Vocabulary section (pp. 101-104) to find key terms and biblical references.

Part II: Focused Reading (pp. 82–88)

How is God Portrayed in the Bible? (pp. 82–85)
Pre-Reading. Since this is not the first time your students have practiced skimming a reading, you may want to ask them to complete steps 2a. and 2b. within a set amount of time (e.g., 2-3 minutes).

Reading. Check to make sure students are following the directions related to using the glosses instead of a dictionary, underlining (or highlighting) only the most important terms or concepts, and writing comments and questions in the margin.

Understanding the Reading. For lower-level students, have them read paragraphs 1-5, pp. 83-84, either working in a small group or in pairs. Then complete the reading, working individually with paragraphs 6-8, p. 84.

Who is God? (pp. 85–88)
Understanding the Reading. Discuss questions 3 and 4 with your students.

Part III: Grammar and Vocabulary (pp. 88–96)

Grammar: Adjective Clauses (pp. 88–91)
Your students have probably studied adjective clauses in their other English classes, although they may have called them by another name, such as *adjectival clause, relative clause, dependent clause,* or *subordinate clause.*

1. If possible, begin your discussion of adjective clauses with a review of information taken from ESL/EFL textbooks your students have used previously.
2. Work through the information and chart on p. 89, using additional examples as needed.
3. In addition to discussing the example on p. 89, you may need to work through two or three more items with your students before they can do this exercise on their own.

4. You may need to give your students additional practice sentences, so that they can easily identify adjective clauses before you move on to contrast adjective clauses with other clauses (p. 89).
5. Follow generally the same procedures with pp. 89–90, working carefully through the information and chart on p. 90 and then helping students with the example and first item or two.

Note that students will continue their work with adjective clauses in Chapter 4 (pp. 121–126). To be successful in the Chapter 4 grammar section, they will need to have a strong foundation in the basic information about adjective clauses in Chapter 3.

Vocabulary: Prefixes (pp. 91–96)
If your students have learned word analysis skills in other English classes, they may have called it *word building* or *the study of word parts*.

Before teaching this section, look ahead to Chapter 4 (pp. 126–129) to see the prefixes covered in that lesson. Note that in *ETE* we do not deal with all English prefixes. Rather, we include only prefixes that occur frequently and also change the meaning of words in ways that are obvious to the reader.

1. You may want to ask students to bring to class any materials they have for prefixes, roots, and suffixes. These materials will not only help you to know what your students have studied previously, but they can provide additional examples and practice exercises.
2. Try to build upon your students' prior knowledge to introduce this section. Even if they have not studied word analysis in another course, they will know some of the most common prefixes, such as *un-, anti-,* and *non-*.
3. You may want to have students work with a partner or in a small group to make a list of as many words as they can think of for prefixes of number (pp. 92–93). Then allow them to use a dictionary to add more words to their lists. Use the same procedure for negative prefixes (pp. 94–95). Check to make sure the words they choose actually contain their prefixes.
4. Work through the information and exercises with your students. Generally they will find these prefixes easy to learn initially, but they may quickly forget the meaning of the prefixes they use less often. This means that frequent review is helpful, as is pointing out prefixes in their readings.

For additional practice exercises, look on the Internet.

Part IV: Focused Reading (pp. 97–100)
Review the procedures you used for earlier Focused Readings, and modify them as needed.

Part V: Theological Vocabulary (pp. 100–105)

Your students have no doubt already discovered that the Focused Readings contain a number of important theological concepts and terms. In addition, beginning with Chapter 3, each chapter of *ETE* includes a major section, Theological Vocabulary, which presents terms commonly found in introductory theology textbooks. Each term is defined in a way that those new to the study of theology can comprehend easily.

Before you assign this section, we suggest that you and your students review the vocabulary learning strategies in the Introduction, pp. 5-8. Ask students to select one new strategy to apply to learning the Chapter 3 Theological Vocabulary.

After completing this section, including the Understanding the Reading exercises, have students use Figure 3.2 (p. 101) to make a list of theological terms that they do not know, or know well. If they need to do so, review the information for making vocabulary cards and making entries in a vocabulary notebook (pp. 9-16). Then have students make vocabulary cards for these words or enter them in their vocabulary notebooks.

Part VI: Review (pp. 106–109)

Review the procedures you used in the Review section of Chapter 1 (*TG*, p. 42), and modify them as needed.

Chapter 4: Revelation

Many of the teaching notes for Chapter 1 (*TG*, pp. 32-42) are equally applicable for Chapter 4. You may want to review those notes before starting to teach this new chapter.

Part I: Vocabulary and Reading Skills (pp. 112–117)

Reading for Meaning (pp. 114–117)

Reading Strategy: Locating the Main Idea, Topic Sentence, and Supporting Details. Before assigning this section, review the relevant Reading for Meaning sections in Chapter 1 (pp. 33-35) and Chapter 3 (pp. 80-81). Be sure your students can locate the main idea in a paragraph and, when appropriate, the topic sentence. The information in this section will build upon what they learned in Chapters 1 and 3.

Since this is a new type of exercise, you will probably need to work through the first item or two with your students. Make sure they understand supporting details and additional information and can locate each one easily. Also, you may need to provide additional paragraphs for practice.

Note that this strategy also occurs in Chapter 5 (pp. 142-145), Chapter 6 (pp. 173-175), and Chapter 7 (pp. 206-207).

Part II: Focused Reading (pp. 117–121)

Review the procedures you used for earlier Focused Readings, and modify them as needed.

This may also be a good time to review selected reading strategies in the Introduction (pp. 1-4) and Chapter 1 (pp. 20-22). Select one or two new strategies for your class (or for each individual) to focus on as they do the Chapter 4 readings.

Part III: Grammar and Vocabulary (pp. 121–129)

Grammar: Adjective Clauses (pp. 121–126)

1. Before assigning this section, review the section on adjective clauses in Chapter 3 (pp. 88-91).
2. Review the procedures you used in Chapter 3 for teaching adjective clauses, and modify them as needed.
3. Since reduced adjective clauses are sometimes difficult to identify, you may want to create some additional exercises or select sentences in the Focused Readings that can be used for identifying reduced adjective clauses.

Vocabulary: Prefixes (pp. 126–129)

1. Before assigning this section, review the section on prefixes in Chapter 3 (pp. 91-96).
2. Review the procedures you used in Chapter 3 for teaching prefixes, and modify them as needed.

Note that Figure 6.2 on p. 201 lists all the prefixes used in the Chapter 3 and Chapter 4 exercises.

Part IV: Theological Vocabulary (pp. 129–133)

1. Review the procedures you used for earlier Theological Vocabulary sections, and modify them as needed.
2. Remind your students to apply one or more of their new vocabulary learning strategies, and then monitor their progress.

Part V: Review (pp. 134–137)

1. Review the procedures you used in earlier Review sections, and modify them as needed.
2. Students should have a number of learning strategies that they have practiced consistently. Have them identify these strategies and discuss their progress in using each one. In addition, you may want to examine your students' ability to apply some of these strategies (e.g., skimming, scanning, outlining, finding the main idea) with a reading passage of your choice.
3. You may want to create an exam to test students' knowledge of key grammar points, prefixes, and theological terms from Chapters 1-4.

Chapter 5: Humanity

Many of the teaching notes for Chapter 1 (*TG*, pp. 32-42) are equally applicable for Chapter 5. You may want to review those notes before starting to teach this new chapter.

Part I: Vocabulary and Reading Skills (pp. 140–145)

Reading for Meaning (pp. 142–145)
Reading Strategy: Learning More About Supporting Details. This section is a continuation from Chapter 4 (pp. 114-117). If necessary, review relevant sections related to main idea, topic sentence and supporting details from Chapters 1 (pp. 33-35) and 4 (pp. 114-117).

Part II: Focused Reading (pp. 145–149)

Review the procedures you used for earlier Focused Readings, and modify them as needed.

Part III: Grammar and Vocabulary (pp. 149–157)

Grammar: Noun Clauses (pp. 149–152)

1. Before assigning this section, review the section on adjective clauses in Chapter 3 (pp. 88-91) and Chapter 4 (pp. 121-126).
2. If possible, begin your discussion of these clauses with a review of information taken from your students' ESL/EFL textbooks.
3. Work through the information and charts on pp. 149-150, using additional examples as needed.
4. In addition to discussing the example provided with each exercise, you may need to work through two or three items with your students before they can do the exercises on their own.

Noun clauses will be reviewed, along with adjective clauses, in Chapter 9 (pp. 281-282).

Vocabulary: Suffixes (pp. 153–157)
This chapter gives an overview of suffixes and presents detailed information about adverb suffixes (e.g., the *-ly* in *carefully, friendly*) and adjective suffixes (e.g., the *-ful* in *faithful* and the *-al* in *natural*). Two additional types, verb suffixes and noun suffixes, are addressed in Chapter 6 (pp. 182-186). Before teaching this section in Chapter 5, look ahead to Chapter 6 to get an overview of material covered in that lesson.

1. You may want to ask students to bring to class any materials they have for prefixes, roots, and suffixes. These materials will not only help you to know what your students have studied previously, but they can provide additional examples and practice exercises.

2. Try to build upon your students' prior knowledge to introduce this section. Even if they have not studied word analysis in another course, they will know many of the common suffixes.

For additional practice exercises, look on the Internet.

Part IV: Focused Reading (pp. 157–161)
Review the procedures you used for earlier Focused Readings, and modify them as needed.

Part V: Theological Vocabulary (pp. 161–164)
Review the procedures you used for earlier Theological Vocabulary sections, and modify them as needed.

Part VI: Review (pp. 164–167)
Review the procedures you used in earlier Review sections, and modify them as needed.

Chapter 6: Jesus Christ
Many of the teaching notes for Chapter 1 (*TG*, pp. 32–42) are equally applicable for Chapter 6. You may want to review those notes before starting to teach this new chapter.

Part I: Vocabulary and Reading Skills (pp. 170–175)

Reading for Meaning (pp. 173–175)
Reading Strategy: Locating the Main Idea and Topic Sentence. This section is a continuation of the explanation and exercises in Chapter 5 (pp. 142–145) regarding identifying the main idea and supporting details. If necessary, review relevant sections related to the main idea, topic sentence, and supporting details from Chapters 1 (pp. 33–35), 4 (pp. 114–117), and 5 (pp. 142–145).

Part II: Focused Reading (pp. 175–181)
Review the procedures you used for earlier Focused Readings, and modify them as needed.

Part III: Vocabulary (pp. 182–186)
This chapter continues the presentation of suffixes. Adverb and adjective suffixes were addressed in Chapter 5 (pp. 153–157). Chapter 6 deals with verb suffixes (e.g., *-ate* in *activate*) and noun suffixes (e.g., *-er* in *teacher*).

1. Before assigning this section, review the section on suffixes in Chapter 5 (pp. 153–157).
2. Review the procedures you used in Chapter 5 for teaching suffixes, and modify them as needed.

Note that Figure 6.3 on p. 202 lists all the suffixes used in the Chapter 5 and Chapter 6 exercises.

Part IV: Focused Reading (pp. 186–191)
Review the procedures you used for earlier Focused Readings, and modify them as needed.

Part V: Theological Vocabulary (pp. 192–198)
Review the procedures you used for earlier Theological Vocabulary sections, and modify them as needed.

Understanding the Reading (p. 197)

1.   Put the hymn by Philip P. Bliss on the board or an overhead transparency.
2.   Read it through aloud. Have students follow in their books.
3.   Give students an example of P (person of Jesus) and W (work of Jesus).
4.   Be sure to review words that may be difficult for students to understand (e.g., *scoffing rude, vile*).
5.   Give students time to do the exercise on their own in class.
6.   Go over the responses as a whole class.

Part VI: Review (pp. 198–202)
Review the procedures you used in earlier Review sections, and modify them as needed.

Chapter 7: Holy Spirit
Many of the teaching notes for Chapter 1 (*TG*, pp. 32–42) are equally applicable for Chapter 7. You may want to review those notes before starting to teach this new chapter.

Part I: Vocabulary and Reading Skills (pp. 204–212)

Reading for Meaning (pp. 206–212)
Reading Strategy: Using Organizational Markers. This section continues the discussion of organizational markers. Chapter 2 (pp. 57–61) covered three types: examples and illustrations, a series of items, and events in a time sequence. This section deals with markers for comparison and contrast as well as markers for cause and effect.

1.   Before teaching this section, review the markers discussed in Chapter 2 (pp. 57–61).
2.   Because this is a long section, you may want to teach comparison and contrast on one day and cause and effect on another day.
3.   Work carefully through the information and examples.

4. You may need to help your students do the first item or two. If needed, find additional exercises in the textbook or other written materials.
5. You can find supplementary exercises on the Internet. Use a search engine such as Google to search for *organizational markers* or *organizational structure* and the specific type of marker, such as *comparison and contrast*.

Part II: Focused Reading (pp. 213–219)

1. Before students do the Focused Reading, The Holy Spirit—His Work (pp. 216-219), have them review the Creed of Constantinople (Ch. 3, p. 87) which addresses the work of the Holy Spirit.
2. Review the procedures you used for earlier Focused Readings, and modify them as needed.

Part III: Focused Reading (pp. 219–222)

Review the procedures you used for earlier Focused Readings, and modify them as needed.

Part IV: Theological Vocabulary (pp. 222–227)

Review the procedures you used for earlier Theological Vocabulary sections, and modify them as needed.

Part V: Review (pp. 227–229)

Review the procedures you used in earlier Review sections, and modify them as needed.

Chapter 8: Salvation and the Christian Life

Chapter 8 marks an important milestone. Beginning with this chapter, we introduce authentic writings from theological publications. Your students should find the excerpts in Chapters 8 and 9 to be only slightly more challenging than the Focused Readings in earlier chapters. If they can read these excerpts with good comprehension, this is a strong indication that they have the requisite language skills for reading theology books and articles written in English.

Many of the teaching notes for Chapter 1 (*TG*, pp. 32-42) are equally applicable for Chapter 8. You may want to review those notes before starting to teach this new chapter.

Part I: Vocabulary and Reading Skills (pp. 232–237)

Reading for Meaning (pp. 236–237)

Reading Strategy: Locating the Main Idea and Supporting Details. This is the final section for locating the main idea and supporting details. If your students find it difficult to identify supporting details, review the relevant sections in Chapter 4 (pp. 114-117), Chapter 5 (pp. 142-145), Chapter 6 (pp. 173-175), and Chapter 7 (pp. 206-207).

Part II: Focused Reading (pp. 238–246)

There are three readings in this section. The first is similar to the Focused Readings in earlier chapters, with glosses in the right margin. However, the next two readings are different in that they are taken from two different theological dictionaries and each has a different author. They also differ in that there are no glosses and there are other minor differences, such as the abbreviations used for the books of the Bible, spelling (e.g., *Savior* in the second reading and *Saviour* in the third), and punctuation.

1. Give special attention to each of the three Pre-Reading sections.
2. Before each reading, pre-teach difficult vocabulary words as needed. This is especially important for the two excerpts from theological dictionaries, where no glosses are provided.
3. For the two excerpts, note that the directions differ from other Focused Readings. In particular, students may need to use a dictionary or theological dictionary.
4. Review the teaching procedures you used for earlier Focused Readings, and modify them as needed. For example, you may want to divide the third reading into two sections.
5. Discuss with your students the advantages of having three readings on the same topic. Points they are likely to mention include the following:
   a. Reading three articles makes it easier to understand the broad topic of salvation.
   b. Each author emphasizes different points, giving a more complete picture than is presented by any one of the three articles.
   c. There is some overlap in vocabulary in the three readings, making it easier to learn new vocabulary.

Part III: Vocabulary (pp. 246–251)

This chapter completes our work on word analysis. Before studying roots (called *word stems* in some publications), you may want to review the earlier sections on prefixes and suffixes (Ch. 3, pp. 91-96, Ch. 4, pp. 126-129, Ch. 5, pp. 153-157, and Ch. 6, pp. 182-186).

The information and practice exercises cover only a small number of the thousands of roots in English. Learning these common roots can help your students expand their vocabulary. However, we believe these exercises on roots have an even more important function, which is to encourage students to notice roots that occur frequently in their reading and to see how the meaning of a root carries over from one word to another. For example, your students have encountered the words *theology, theological,* and *theologian* many times in *ETE*. If they know that the root *the(o)-* means "God," this should help them figure out the meaning of other words with the same root: *thearchy, theocentric, theocracy, theocrat, theodicy, theody, theomania,* and even *atheist.* Likewise, if they know the root *mor(t)-,* which refers to death, this should help them figure out the meaning of *mortal, mortality, mortally, mortician, mortify, mortuary, immortality,* and *immortalize.*

Part IV: Focused Reading (pp. 252–257)
Review the procedures you used for the Focused Readings on pp. 238-246, and modify them as needed.

Part V: Theological Vocabulary (pp. 257–265)
Review the procedures you used for earlier Theological Vocabulary sections, and modify them as needed.

Part VI: Review (pp. 265–267)
Review the procedures you used in earlier Review sections, and modify them as needed.

Chapter 9: Church
Many of the teaching notes for Chapter 1 (*TG*, pp. 32-42) are equally applicable for Chapter 9. You may want to review those notes before starting to teach this new chapter.

Part I: Vocabulary and Reading Skills (pp. 270–274)

Reading for Meaning (pp. 272–274)
Reading Strategy: SQ3R. Be sure your students get sufficient practice in using SQ3R, which is a very powerful reading strategy that will help them not only with their theological reading but with all academic reading in English and in their native language.

Seymour and Walsh (2006, 73) discuss a similar multi-step procedure called "muscle reading."

Step 1:	Preview	look for concepts, charts, titles
Step 2:	Outline	make an outline
Step 3:	Question	turn titles and headings into questions
Step 4:	Read	stay focused
Step 5:	Underline	underline or highlight sparingly, write notes in the margin
Step 6:	Answer	answer questions made in step 3
Step 7:	Recite	talk to yourself about the reading
Step 8:	Review	do in the first 24 hours
Step 9:	Review	weekly or monthly

Part II: Focused Reading (pp. 274–280)

1. The two readings in this section contain a number of vocabulary items that may be especially challenging for your students. We suggest that you identify these words before assigning each reading.

You may want to have your students scan the readings in order to make a list (or two lists, one for each reading) of words they do not know. Then pre-teach the key vocabulary.

2. Review the procedures you used for earlier Focused Readings, and modify them as needed.

Part III: Grammar (pp. 281–285)
This section contains no new information and should not be difficult for your students.

Part IV: Theological Vocabulary (pp. 285–295)
Review the procedures you used for earlier Theological Vocabulary sections, and modify them as needed.

Part VI: Review (pp. 295–298)
Review the procedures you used in earlier Review sections, and modify them as needed.

Chapter 10: Last Things
Many of the teaching notes for Chapter 1 (*TG*, pp. 32-42) are equally applicable for Chapter 10. You may want to review those notes before starting to teach this new chapter.

Part I: Vocabulary and Reading Skills (pp. 300–303)

Reading for Meaning (p. 303)
Reading Strategy: Understanding Articles in Theological Dictionaries. This section provides a study procedure adapted from the SQ3R strategy. We suggest that you have your students use it for most or even all of the Focused Readings in Chapter 10.

Part II: Focused Reading (pp. 304–318)

1. The Focused Readings on eschatology are quite long and also difficult to understand. Before each of the three readings, we have provided a pre-reading exercise to teach some of the more challenging vocabulary. However, you may want to pre-teach additional vocabulary items to your students.
2. Review the procedures you used for earlier Focused Readings, and modify them as needed.

Part III: Theological Vocabulary (pp. 319–327)
Review the procedures you used for earlier Theological Vocabulary sections, and modify them as needed.

Part IV: Review (pp. 328–329)

Review the procedures you used in earlier Review sections, and modify them as needed.

Final Thoughts

This final reading should be much easier for your students to comprehend than the Chapter 10 dictionary article on eschatology. It offers encouragement to students to apply their biblical and theological knowledge to their daily decisions as Christians.

Answer Key

This section contains answers to the exercises in the Introduction through Chapter 10 of *ETE*. For many items there is only one correct answer, but for others there is more than one acceptable response. For these you will see "Answers may vary." For some items with more than one correct response, you will find suggested answers.

Introduction

Planning Your Learning (p. 2)
Answers may vary.

Managing Your Learning (pp. 3–4)
1. a. sanctified: made holy
   b. justified: made right with God
2. a. weak, shaky
   b. other people
   c. to be disabled, to fall, to get worse

Expanding Your Learning (p. 4)
Answers may vary.

Figuring Out Word Meanings (pp. 5–6)
1. a. modalism: an endeavor to explain the Trinity; one God, three different roles; likened to one person who is a son, father, and shopkeeper
   b. consummation: the finalization of God's restoration and victory
   c. mourn: the opposite of celebrate with joy
2. a. verb, noun
   b. noun, verb
3.
sug**gest**ion	under**lie**	**diction**ary
re**establish**	**text**ual	**strength**en
para**phrase**	re**store**	**individ**ually
s**ymbo**lic	en**able**	super**natural**

Exercises (p. 8)

1. 1. plead; 2. compelling; 3. strategy; 4. lineage; 5. kneel; 6. distort; 7. enthroned; 8. disciples

2. 1. total depravity; 2. justice; 3. worldview; 4. illumination; 5. glossolalia; 6. omnipresent; 7. crucifixion; 8. exegesis

Exercise (p. 9)

Answers may vary.

1. skimming: looking over a reading passage quickly to find the main ideas
2. justice: God treats all people with fairness, according to his perfect law
3. learning strategy: techniques, procedures, or steps you take to help yourself learn more effectively, such as reading and vocabulary strategies
4. soteriology: the study of theology that deals with salvation

Exercise (p. 10)

Answers may vary.

Exercise (p. 11)

1.	permeate	general vocabulary
2.	providence	general vocabulary with theological meaning
3.	initial	general vocabulary
4.	sustainer	general vocabulary with theological meaning
5.	adoption	general vocabulary with theological meaning
6.	omnipotence	theological vocabulary
7.	hermeneutics	general vocabulary with theological meaning
8.	mediator	general vocabulary with theological meaning
9.	ignorance	general vocabulary

Exercise (pp. 11–12)

Answers may vary.

Chapter 1

Pre-Reading (p. 22)

1. The purpose is to understand the different areas of interpreting the biblical text.
2. Answers may vary.
3. Answers may vary.

Understanding the Reading (pp. 28–29)

1. 1. d; 2. g; 3. h; 4. c; 5. k; 6. j; 7. i; 8. e; 9. b; 10. a; 11. f

2. Answers may vary. To "go there" means to enter the world of the Bible in order to understand the original meaning of a biblical text, and to "come back again" means to return to our context in order to apply what we learned from that text.

3. Answers may vary.

4. Language: textual criticism, linguistics, philology, grammar (syntax), translation

   Introductory/Critical and Literary Issues: author, recipients, date, purpose, situation, literary form (genre), sources

   Background: historical, cultural, geographical, intellectual, philosophical, religious, social

   Interpretation: hermeneutics, exegesis

   Theology: historical, biblical, systematic, practical

Word Forms (p. 30)

1. created (v); 2. illustration (n); 3. definition (n); 4. assumptions (n); 5. interpret (v)

Fill in the Blank (p. 31)

1. task; 2. unique; 3. involves; 4. variations; 5. assumes; 6. aware; 7. theory; 8. distinct; 9. version; 10. author; 11. individual

Vocabulary in Context (p. 32)

1. c; 2. b; 3. c; 4. c; 5. a; 6. b; 7. a; 8. c; 9. c; 10. a

Word Families in Context (p. 33)

Paragraph 1: 1. creation; 2. Creator; 3. created; 4. creative

Paragraph 2: 1. translate; 2. translators; 3. translating; 4. translations

Exercises (pp. 34–35)

1.   1. c; 2. a
2.   1. b; 2. a
3.   1. b; 2. a

Exercises (pp. 36–37)

1. a. The Worldview of Biblical Writers

   b. The worldview of the biblical writers is represented in four broad phases. The subject will be how the worldview of the biblical writers is revealed throughout the Bible.

   c. Answers may vary. It discusses the biblical writers' worldview in four phases. Each phase is described in detail.

   d. Answers may vary. The fact that the worldview of the biblical writers sees history moving toward God's goal of restoration and victory.

e. Answers may vary. Some terms are creation, transcendent, sovereign, fall, sin, redemption, and consummation.

2. A. Creation
   B. Fall
   C. Process of redemption and restoration
   D. Consummation

Pre-Reading (p. 37)

1. N; 2. N; 3. B; 4. N; 5. B; 6. N; 7. B

Understanding the Reading (p. 39)

1. 1. CON; 2. F; 3. PRR; 4. CR; 5. CON; 6. CR; 7. CON; 8. F; 9. CON; 10. F; 11. PRR; 12. F

2. Answers may vary.

Pre-Reading (p. 40)

1. Answers may vary. The reading explains different types of Bible translations from the original biblical languages of Hebrew, Aramaic, and Greek.

2. literal (formal equivalent), paraphrase (free translation), functional (dynamic) equivalent

3. Answers may vary.

Understanding the Reading (pp. 43–44)

1. Hebrew, Aramaic, Greek

2. The two issues are having access to the best possible texts, and determining how to translate most accurately and clearly the words and ideas from one language to another.

3. The literal (formal equivalent) translation remains as close as possible to the exact word and sentence structure of the original language while the functional (dynamic) equivalent translation modernizes the language, grammar, and style.

4. The functional (dynamic) equivalent translation tries to maintain the original references to matters of history and culture while the paraphrase is willing to eliminate much of the historical distance between the ancient setting of the Bible and the setting of the contemporary reader.

5. It is helpful to use more than one English translation of the Bible because no single translation can capture the full meaning of the text in its original language.

Reviewing Theological Vocabulary (pp. 44–45)

1. b; 2. d; 3. c; 4. a; 5. b; 6. a; 7. b; 8. c; 9. c; 10. d; 11. a; 12. a

Comparing Translations (pp. 46–47)

Answers may vary.

1 John 2:1b–2a

1. NLT: Col. 2, Col. 4: explains "advocate" and "propitiation"
2. TEV: Col. 2, Col. 3, Col. 4: explains "advocate" and "propitiation"
3. CEV: Col. 1, Col. 2, Col. 3, Col. 4: explains "righteous," "advocate," and "propitiation"
4. NLV: Col. 1, Col. 2, Col. 3, Col. 4: explains "advocate," righteous," and "propitiation"

Philippians 2:13

1. NIV: Col. 4: "purpose" instead of "pleasure"
2. NLT: Col. 1, Col. 4: explains "will" and "good pleasure"
3. TEV: Col. 1, Col. 4: adverb "always" added, "purpose" instead of "pleasure"
4. CEV: Col. 1, Col. 2, Col 4: "able to obey" instead of "good pleasure"
5. NLV: Col. 1, Col. 2, Col 4: "helping you obey" instead of "will," explains "good pleasure"

Understanding Learning Strategies (pp. 47–48)

Answers may vary for rewritten items.

1. FALSE: Look quickly over the text for the most important ideas.
2. FALSE: Scanning is helpful in locating specific information in a reading passage.
3. FALSE: Overuse of a dictionary can slow down the reading process and discourage the development of other important reading skills.
4. TRUE
5. FALSE: Focus on phrases or small groups of words that belong together. This helps you read more quickly and understand more of what you read.
6. TRUE
7. TRUE
8. FALSE: Those who practice frequent review will be more likely to remember the main points and much of the supporting detail in a text.
9. TRUE

Evaluating Your Learning (p. 48)

Answers may vary.

Chapter 2

Pre-Reading (p. 50)

Answers may vary. Theology in its broadest sense is the study of God in relationship to humankind. It also refers to the study of God.

Understanding the Reading (p. 51)

1. Answers may vary. Theology comes from two Greek words: *theos* (God) and *logos* (word, reason, speech). This reading has expanded my understanding in terms of the nature and activity of God, about human beings who are his creation, and about all that exists within the universe as well as his reconciling work through Jesus Christ.

    Christian theology is an organized study of God and his relationship with humankind. It's about the nature and activity of God, about humankind, the universe, and his work to reconcile people back to himself. Christian theology is based on the Scriptures, but other areas such as the historical study of theology and philosophy may be referred to in the study.

Pre-Reading (p. 52)

1. historical, biblical, systematic, and practical
2. an investigation of the four types of theology

Understanding the Reading (p. 54)

1. P; 2. B; 3. H; 4. S; 5. S; 6. B; 7. S; 8. P; 9. S; 10. P; 11. H; 12. B; 13. H

Fill in the Blank (p. 55)

1. reject, verb; 2. significant, adjective; 3. specific, adjective; 4. traditionally, adverb; 5. concept, noun; 6. logic, noun

Vocabulary in Context (pp. 55–56)

1. a; 2. a; 3. b; 4. b; 5. b; 6. b; 7. a; 8. c; 9. b

Word Definitions (p. 56)

Answers may vary.

1. final: the last visit
2. affect: make a difference
3. primary: of chief importance
4. guideline: a general principle
5. available: able to be obtained
6. objective: an aim or goal
7. achieve: reach or attain
8. significant: noteworthy, important, to be worthy of attention

Word Families in Context (p. 57)

Paragraph 1: 1. theology; 2. theological; 3. theologians; 4. theologically
Paragraph 2: 1. systematic; 2. system; 3. systematize; 4. systematically

Exercises (p. 58)

1. a. specifically
   b. that is
2. a. e.g., for example
   b. such as, for example

Exercises (pp. 59–60)

1. first, final, a, b
2. begins, ends, between
3. to begin with, moreover, additional
4. Another clue is the repetition of "God" in each part of the series: "God has revealed," "God manifests," and "God's disclosure."
5. Historical theology investigates Christian thought . . . (¶ 2)
   Another framework . . . is called biblical theology. (¶ 3)
   A third major branch of theology is systematic theology . . . (¶ 4)
   The last major branch . . . is practical theology. (¶ 5)
6. dictionaries: the English-only dictionary, the bilingual dictionary, the ESL/EFL learner's dictionary, and the theological dictionary
7. (3) discusses some key issues over which theologians differ
   (4) discusses the organization of paragraphs
   (5) introduces the use of organizational markers that help readers understand theological writing
   (6) describes different types of dictionaries
   (7) lists a number of theological dictionaries
   (8) provides practice exercises in their use
8. First series: identify, define, and explain
   Second series: topics, terms, names, places
   Third series: theological textbooks, journals, and other scholarly writings

Exercises (p. 61)

1. a. eventually
   b. at the same time
   c. eventually
   d. at the time
2. a. first, then
   b. later, earlier
   c. while, simultaneously
3. before, then, during, again
4. first, then, as, begin, while, before, begin, when, then

Exercise (p. 62)

Answers may vary. Sample outline:

II. **Biblical Theology**

   A.   Study of Bible in its original historical-cultural setting

   B.   Learn to understand Bible in its own context

   1.   Let Bible speak its own message

   2.   Aware of God's revelation through his words and works in various contexts

   3.   Guideline for understanding Bible's message in other cultures

III. **Systematic Theology**

   A.   Study of teachings of Bible in logical, orderly manner

   B.   Two approaches

   1.   Organize biblical data into categories

   a.   Understand biblical data and relationships among its parts

   b.   Refer to as Christian doctrines

   2.   Look at biblical teaching as a coherent whole

   a.   Provides order and logic in organization

   b.   Facilitates applying biblical message to contemporary world

IV. **Practical Theology**

   A.   Study of relating theology to ministry, proclaiming, teaching, and living Christian life

   B.   Ministry methods in harmony with God and Christian faith

   1.   Base on biblical and theological principles

   2.   Recognize sinful nature of human beings

   3.   Understand power of gospel

Exercises (pp. 66–67)

1.   1. Entry word: Judgment Seat

   2. Word in its original language: Greek word *bema*

   3. Definition: literally a "step," referring to platform

   4. Biblical references: Acts 18:12, 16; John 19:13; and Acts 25:23

   5. Abbreviations: none

   6. Bibliography: J. Bailey, *And Life Everlasting,* etc.

   7. Authorship: S. E. McClelland

   8. Cross-references: Judgment, Judgment of the Nations, Last Judgment

2.   1. Entry word: logos

   2. Word in its original language: Greek word *logos*

   3. Definition: A title for Christ

   4. Biblical references: John 1:1, 14

   5. Abbreviations: OT

6. Bibliography: none

7. Authorship: none

8. Cross-references: Christology, Jesus, Word, Word of God, Word of the Lord

3.   Answers may vary.

4.   Answers may vary.

Pre-Reading (p. 68)

Three intellectual issues are theology and history, ideas about the nature of Christianity, and supernaturalism and naturalism.

Understanding the Reading (pp. 70–72)

2.   Answers may vary. Sample outline:

    I.   **Theology and History**

        A.   Opposing views of what history is

            1.   Biblical history reports what really happened

            2.   Biblical history may or may not be true or important

        B.   Theological use of German words for "history"

            1.   *Historie*

            2.   *Geschichte*

    II.   **Ideas About the Nature of Christianity**

        A.   Traditional view

            1.   God's actions and human response

            2.   Response should be one of faith

        B.   Old liberal view (modernism)

            1.   Focus on humans, not God

            2.   Involves human effort for progress and improvement

        C.   Contemporary non-evangelical view (theology of existence)

            1.   Focus on human attainment of self-awareness

            2.   Goal is to find meaning and purpose

    III.   **Supernaturalism and Naturalism**

        A.   The Enlightenment

            1.   Human reason, the scientific method, and autonomy

            2.   Rejection of the supernatural

        B.   Application for studies

            1.   Be aware of author's presuppositions

            2.   Need to distinguish truth from error

3.   1. T; 2. N; 3. N; 4. T; 5. T; 6. T or S; 7. S

5.   1.   presuppositions: a person's underlying assumptions or beliefs about something

        2.   *historie:* a German term referring to events which happened in time and place and which are verifiable

3. *geschichte:* a German term which refers to significant reports of the past which have an impact upon people in the present

4. verifiable: events that can be proved to have actually taken place

5. the Enlightenment: an intellectual movement where human reason, the scientific method, and autonomy became very important

Understanding Reading Skills (pp. 72–73)

1. Answer may vary for rewritten items.
    1. TRUE
    2. TRUE
    3. FALSE: Organizational markers for examples and illustrations include "that is," "for example," and "specifically."
    4. TRUE
    5. FALSE: Frequently, a series is not introduced with markers.
    6. TRUE
    7. FALSE: When outlining, include only the information you want to remember.
    8. FALSE: Once you have learned something well, review it frequently.
    9. TRUE
    10. FALSE: Organizational markers for events in a time sequence or steps in a process include "eventually" and "before," but not "for example."
2. Answers may vary.

Using Theological Dictionaries (p. 74)

Answers may vary.

Reviewing Theological Vocabulary (pp. 75–76)

1. b; 2. a; 3. c; 4. c; 5. a; 6. c; 7. d; 8. a; 9. d; 10. d

Evaluating Your Learning (p. 76)

Answers may vary.

Chapter 3

Word Selection (p. 78)

1. visible; 2. sustains; 3. various; 4. capable; 5. identifying; 6. acknowledge; 7. rely

Vocabulary in Context (pp. 78–79)

1. c; 2. a; 3. c; 4. a; 5. b; 6. b; 7. c

Dictionary Use (p. 79)

Answers may vary.

1. accurate: free from error, exact
2. conclude: to bring to an end, to finish
3. consequently: as a result
4. emphasize: to give special importance to
5. initial: first or immediate
6. reveal: to make known, to show

Word Families in Context (p. 80)

Paragraph 1: 1. just; 2. judge; 3. justice; 4. justifies
Paragraph 2: 1. true; 2. truly; 3. truthfulness; 4. truthful

Exercises (pp. 80–81)

1. 1. a; 2. a
2. 1. c; 2. b

Exercises (p. 82)

1. Gen 1:1; Ps 104; Mt 5:45; Rom 8:38–39; Gen 3; Eph 1:3–14; Rom 3:21–30
2. 1. ¶ 4; 2. ¶ 3; 3. ¶ 5; 4. ¶ 7; 5. ¶ 6

Pre-Reading (pp. 82–83)

1. Answers may vary.
2. a. Title: How is God Portrayed in the Bible?
        Subheadings: Creator, Sustainer, Redeemer/Reconciler, Judge
    b. understanding how God is portrayed in the Bible
    c. Answers may vary. Examples: Creator, creation, *ex nihilo,* reverence,
        worship, obedience, consummation, providence, realm, restore,
        predestined, justifies, Theology Proper

Understanding the Reading (p. 85)

Answers may vary.

1. Creator: God is Maker of heaven and earth. The climax of his creation is
    humankind whom he made in his own image. As Creator, he has the right to
    establish principles, both moral and ethical for us to follow.
    Sustainer: God continues his involvement in his created order. He supports it
    and guides it toward the purposes he intended.
    Redeemer/Reconciler: God provided a way through Jesus Christ to restore his
    creation to a proper relationship with himself and with others.
    Judge: God administers justice in absolute fairness. His justice for
    wrongdoing and his offer of redemption through Jesus Christ work hand in
    hand.
2. Providence means that God takes care of his creation. It portrays God's
    sovereignty over the universe and also his personal care of human beings.
    As Sustainer, God is involved with his creation. His providential care over

humankind demonstrates his active involvement with his children, and nothing happens in our lives by chance.

Pre-Reading (pp. 85–86)

1. Who is God?, no subheadings
2. Answers may vary. Example: the personal identity of our triune God
3. Answers may vary. Examples: trinity, triune, modalism

Understanding the Reading (pp. 87–88)

Answers may vary.

1. Trinity is the belief in one God in three distinct persons: God the Father, God the Son, and God the Holy Spirit; equal in divine nature and possessing the same attributes.
2. Modalism teaches that the Trinity is one God who acts in three different roles, such as a person who is a father, a son, and a shopkeeper. Modalism is in error because it fails to say that the Father, Son, and Holy Spirit are three separate distinct persons in one God.
3. Since it's hard for humans to understand the everyday occurrences in nature such as the hatching of a robin's egg why is it so hard to accept that we cannot understand completely the mystery of the Trinity? We are finite and cannot fully comprehend everything about God, who is infinite (unlimited).
4. The Creed of Constantinople is a confession of faith, written by the early church fathers, that expresses essential beliefs about the Trinity, which is the belief in one God in three persons: the Father, the Son, and the Holy Spirit.

Exercise (p. 89)

1. He is both "just and the (one) who justifies."
2. It represents a biblical (doctrine) which permeates every aspect of God's relationship with his creation.
   Alternate answer: (biblical doctrine)
3. ". . . nor anything else in all creation will be able to separate us from the (love) of God that is in Christ Jesus our Lord."
   Alternate answer: (love of God)
4. God has the right to rule over and make requirements of (those) whom he created.
5. Not only does the Bible portray God as the Supreme Being but also as (one) who is a personal being.
6. (Those) who are his people are to reflect his character.
7. Over and over we see concrete (ways) in which God cares for his creation.
   Alternate answer: (concrete ways)
8. There are three (attributes) of God which are classified under the characteristic of integrity and which refer to the matter of truth.
   Alternate answer: (attributes of God)

9. Providence is the(assurance) that God is present and active in our lives and that nothing happens simply by chance.

10. The church was finally able to state the doctrine of the Trinity in a(way) that protected it from the(dangers) that had plagued it in the past.

Exercises (pp. 90–91)

1. 1. Christians maintain that the Bible portrays the one God as three distinct persons. Other

2. The group realized that they had an answer to their question. Other

3. The attributes of God are essential(qualities) which characterize his nature. AC

4. They are permanent(qualities) that cannot be gained or lost. AC

5. They help to define who God is in himself. Other

6. God is not the(sort of being) who can be limited to one location. AC

7. He is like the(wind) which moves but cannot be seen. AC

2. 1. This, his personal(name) by which he identifies himself regularly in the Old Testament (AC) and to which Jesus himself referred, (AC) implies that he is the living and true God. (Other)
Alternate answer:(personal name)

2. The(God) who is genuinely true (AC) and who tells the truth (AC) also proves himself to be true to his faithfulness. That God keeps all his promises (Other) is shown over and over again in Scripture.

3. The early church believed that the Bible, especially the New Testament, teaches the existence, personality, full deity, and unity of the one God who is Father, Son, and Holy Spirit. (Other)
There is an adjective clause within the clause underlined above: . . . of the one(God) who is Father, Son, and Holy Spirit. (AC)

4. The most fundamental teaching of the Bible is that God exists (Other) and that he is the(Supreme Being) (Other) who is ultimately in control of the universe. (AC)

Exercises (p. 93)

1. 1. trip, no prefix; 2. unilateral, one, single; 3. bifocals, two; 4. seminar, no prefix; 5. monotone, one; 6. multigroup, many, more than two; 7. polygamy, many, more than two; 8. bid, no prefix; 9. polyglot, many, more than two; 10. trioxide, three

2. 1. uni; 2. bi; 3. tri; 4. mono; 5. bi; 6. tri; 7. multi, poly; 8. mono; 9. bi; . multi; 11. mono; 12. tri; 13. poly

Exercises (pp. 95–96)

1. 1. unholy; 2. misprint; 3. non-Christian, un-Christian, or anti-Christian; 4. malfunction; 5. anti-war; 6. misbehave; 7. disadvantage; 8. misapply; 9. unbelievable; 10. malnutrition; 11. anti-poverty; 12. discontinue; 13. unlikely; 14. disagree; 15. nonscientific or unscientific; 16. nonsense

2. 1. immobile; 2. insensitive; 3. irregular; 4. impersonal; 5. illegible; 6. infinite;
    7. immoral; 8. irreverent; 9. immortal; 10. inaction; 11. infallible;
    12. irresistible; 13. irredeemable; 14. impatient; 15. illegitimate; 16. injustice
3. 1. j; 2. h; 3. a; 4. k; 5. b; 6. m; 7. c; 8. e; 9. g; 10. d; 11. i; 12. l; 13. f
4. Answers may vary.

Pre-Reading (p. 97)

Answers may vary. Examples:
1. good, powerful, holy, just, love
2. It discusses the question "What is God like?" These characteristics are called attributes.

Understanding the Reading (p. 98)

Answers may vary. Attributes are permanent qualities or characteristics.

Pre-Reading (p. 98)

Answers may vary. Examples:
1. God created the universe but does not intervene in everyday human affairs.
    If I'm good enough, God will let me into heaven.
2. It could create an incorrect understanding of who God is and how he acts.

Understanding the Reading (p. 100)

Answers may vary.
1. heresy: a belief or teaching that is against what the Bible or correct theology teaches
2. immanence: God is present and active within his creation and works in and through natural processes
3. pantheism: everything is God; God and nature are seen as one reality
4. transcendence: God is himself distinct, or radically different from his creation; he is far above and much greater than anything that is created
5. deism: the belief that God created the world but has since left it alone; he set it in motion but does not get involved

Pre-Reading (p. 100)

1. Answers may vary.
2. great, awesome, absolute, unlimited, unrestricted
3. loving, can be trusted, moral qualities, integrity, love

Understanding the Reading (pp. 102–103)

1. 1. immutability; 2. omnipotence; 3. spirit; 4. infinitude; 5. omnipresence;
    6. person; 7. eternity; 8. omniscience
2. 1. Spirit; 2. Omnipotence; 3. Life; 4. Omniscience; 5. Omnipresence;
    6. Eternity; 7. Person

Understanding the Reading (p. 105)

1. 1. grace; 2. genuineness; 3. benevolence; 4. persistence; 5. holiness;
    6. faithfulness; 7. righteousness; 8. justice; 9. mercy
2. 1. Righteousness; 2. Mercy; 3. Persistence; 4. Justice; 5. Holiness;
    6. Faithfulness; 7. Genuineness; 8. Love; 9. Grace; 10. Veracity

Reviewing the Attributes of God (p. 106)

1. 1. merciful; 2. faithful; 3. just; 4. omnipresent; 5. pure; 6. truthful;
    7. righteous; 8. infinite; 9. omniscient; 10. immutable; 11. genuine;
    12. omnipotent; 13. loving; 14. holy; 15. gracious; 16. benevolent;
    17. personal; 18. persistent; 19. eternal; 20. spiritual
2. Answers may vary.

Understanding Reading Skills (p. 107)

Answers may vary.

Reviewing Adjective Clauses (p. 107)

1. The (God) whom we worship is great and awesome.
2. One of the (attributes) of God which describes his greatness is his infinitude.
    Alternate answer: (attributes of God)
3. Moses is the (writer) whose song of deliverance is recorded in Exodus 15.
4. Those (attributes) that refer to God's goodness are his moral purity, integrity
    and love.
5. Paul is the (one) to whom God gave the call to go and preach the gospel to
    the Gentiles.
6. The three (attributes) to which he referred in his sermon are God's
    genuineness, truth, and faithfulness.

Reviewing Word Analysis and Prefixes (pp. 107–108)

Answers may vary for rewritten items.

1. TRUE
2. FALSE: Words may have more than one root.
3. TRUE
4. TRUE
5. FALSE: Prefixes usually change the meaning of the word, and suffixes
    often indicate the part of speech.
6. TRUE
7. TRUE
8. FALSE: *Tribe* is a word that begins with letters that are the same as
    those of the prefix, but it does not have a prefix.
9. TRUE
10. FALSE: The meaning of the prefix *in-* has two different meanings, one
    of which is "not."

Reviewing Theological Vocabulary (pp. 108–109)

1. c; 2. b; 3. d; 4. c; 5. a; 6. b; 7. d; 8. b; 9. d; 10. c; 11. b; 12. d

Evaluating Your Learning (p. 109)

Answers may vary.

Chapter 4

Word Selection (p. 112)

1. somewhat; 2. error; 3. liberal; 4. authority; 5. require; 6. factors; 7. constitute;
8. consists

Word Forms (pp. 112–113)

1. authority, noun; 2. display, verb; 3. insightful, adjective; 4. initiated, verb;
5. liberally, adverb; 6. participation, noun; 7. resourceful, adjective; 8. style, noun

Word Definitions (p. 113)

Answers may vary.

1. surveyed: looked carefully and thoroughly at the city
2. designer: one who plans or creates something with purpose
3. finite: limited, bound by time and space
4. resources: abilities, means
5. initiated: caused the beginning of, started
6. communicate: convey information about himself
7. insight: capacity to understand something or someone
8. participation: taking part in the process
9. style: distinctive way of writing
10. deny: refuse to acknowledge

Word Families in Context (p. 114)

Paragraph 1: 1. revelation; 2. reveals; 3. reveal; 4. revealing

Paragraph 2: 1. inspiration; 2. inspired; 3. inspire; 4. inspirational

Exercises (pp. 114–117)

1. 1. sup. details: He is our Savior; He is the Holy Spirit
   2. Why must we worship God as a triune God?
2. 1. main idea: a; sup. detail: d; additional info.: c
   2. *Exploring Theological English* is an ESL/EFL textbook designed to help you become more proficient at reading theological publications written in English.
3. 1. sup. detail: e; additional info: d, f

2. Another controversy regarding the New Testament canon is the role of the church in the canonical process.

4. 1. main idea: a

   2. During his second missionary journey Paul found himself in the great city of Athens.

   3. main idea: a; sup. details: b, c, d, e, f, g

Pre-Reading (p. 117)

Answers may vary.

Understanding the Reading (p. 118)

1. Sample outline:

   How Can We Know God?

   I. How can we know God?

       A. Doctrine of revelation

           1. Revealed through creation, providence, and history

           2. Revealed through the Bible

   II. Why can't we know God apart from revelation?

       A. God is distinct from humankind

           1. Exists apart from us as Creator

           2. His creation is dependent upon him for existence

           3. Unlimited (infinite) vs. limited (finite)

           4. Knowledge of God beyond our ability to discover

       B. Humankind are sinners

           1. Impairs ability to know God

           2. Affects all humanity

           3. Dependent on God to reveal himself

   III. What does God reveal to us?

       A. God tells us about himself

           1. Who he is

           2. What he has done

           3. What he is doing

           4. What he will do

       B. God tells us about ourselves

           1. We are made to be in relationship with him

           2. He confronts us with himself

           3. He calls us to respond in trust and obedience

2. Answers may vary.

Pre-Reading (p. 119)

General revelation is knowledge of God that is available to all people, at all times, and in all places.

Special revelation is knowledge of God that is available to particular people at particular times and places.

In the traditional use of the term, progressive revelation means that God initiated the revelation of himself, but he did not reveal everything about himself all at once.

Understanding the Reading (pp. 120–121)

1. General revelation is knowledge of God that is available to all people, at all times, and in all places. God revealed himself through nature, human history, human moral conscience, and an innate awareness of a Supreme Being in each human.

2. We need more than general revelation because sin has obscured and in some cases nearly extinguished the light God has given us.

3. personal: God reveals himself to us; redemptive: God restores the broken relationship between us and himself

4. Adam, Noah, Abraham, Isaac, Jacob, Joseph, and the prophets

5. Progressive revelation means that God initiated the revelation of himself, but did not reveal everything all at once.

6. God has revealed himself most completely through his Son, Jesus Christ, who came as a human being, made his dwelling place among us and gave himself up for our salvation.

Review Exercise (p. 121)

1. We are the (creatures) who depend on him for our very existence.
2. . . . a gradual (process) which has moved toward a fuller and more complete form . . .
3. Yet (those) who do hold to the inspiration of Scripture . . .
4. . . . an innate awareness of a (Being) on whom we depend.
5. It is the (doctrine) of revelation that answers this question.
   Alternate answer: (doctrine of revelation)

Exercise (p. 122)

restrictive clauses: who had risen from the dead; who has made himself known; who made the world and everything in it; who left nothing to chance; who created and sustains all; who will judge all

non-restrictive clauses: whose favorite pastime was to discuss new ideas; which had been established to oversee religious and moral matters

Exercise (pp. 123–124)

1. a; 2. b; 3. b; 4. a; 5. b; 6. b

Exercise (pp. 125–126)

1. We have many (translations) (that are, which are) <u>written in easy-to-understand contemporary English.</u>

2. Inspiration is the (method) (that is, which is) <u>employed by God</u> to preserve his message.

3. He sustains his creation and guides it toward the (purposes) (that, which) <u>he intended for it.</u>

4. Sanctification is the continuing work of the (Holy Spirit) (who is) <u>designated as the Spirit of truth,</u> in the life of the believer.

5. You may read theological (writing) (that represents, which represents) <u>representing different theological viewpoints.</u>
   Alternate answer: (theological writing)

6. Systematic theology appeals to (forms) of logic (that are, which are) <u>familiar to the contemporary mind.</u>
   Alternate answer: (forms of logic)

7. God is the (Creator) (who is) <u>transcendent in his being</u> . . .

8. He is supreme in (all) (that) <u>he is and does.</u>

9. Illumination of the Holy Spirit is needed because of (limitations) (that result, which result) <u>resulting from human sinfulness.</u>

10. Practical theology is more than biblical (doctrine) (that is, which is) <u>applied to everyday life.</u>
    Alternate answer: (biblical doctrine)

11. It is important to interpret a literary form in a (manner) (that is, which is) <u>appropriate to that form.</u>

12. "I am the voice of (one) (who is) <u>calling in the desert</u> . . . (Jn 1:23)

13. We do not possess any original biblical (manuscripts) (that were, which were) <u>written by their authors.</u>
    Alternate answer: (biblical manuscripts)

14. Special revelation is (knowledge) of God (that is, which is) <u>available to particular people at particular times and places.</u>
    Alternate answer: (knowledge of God)

15. our (Father) (who is) <u>in heaven.</u>

Exercises (pp. 127–129)

1. 1. <u>Ex</u>communication: removal from the church
   2. <u>neo</u>evangelical: a new form of the evangelical movement
   3. <u>Inter</u>testamental: the period between the testaments
   4. <u>Post</u>modernism: after modernism
      <u>over</u>turns: turn or throw over
   5. <u>re</u>born: be born again
   6. <u>super</u>natural: beyond or above natural events
   7. <u>pre</u>tribulation: before the tribulation

8.   co-exist: to exist together

9.   overtaxed: to tax too much

2.   Answers may vary.

1.   reclassify; to classify again; He will reclassify the rock samples.

2.   overburden; to burden too much; The leaders overburden the people with taxes.

3.   underclass; class below; The slum-dwellers are considered to be the underclass of society.

4.   subcategory; categorize under; Differential equations is a subcategory of calculus.

5.   predestination; destine before; Predestination refers to the sovereign determination of God.

6.   neo-orthodox; a new period of orthodoxy; Neo-orthodoxy comes from three Greek words: neo, ortho, and dokein.

7.   intermediary; mediator or go-between; Christ is the intermediary between God and humankind.

8.   transfiguration; a change in form; Peter, James, and John were not permitted to discuss Christ's transfiguration with the other disciples.

3.   Answers may vary.

1.	predict	I predict that you will finish this course.
2.	exodus	The exodus of God's people from slavery was miraculous.
3.	outcome	The outcome of the trial was a surprise to everyone.
4.	regeneration	Regeneration is the beginning of new life in Christ.
5.	interdenominational	The Bible school is interdenominational.
6.	coexist	The two countries will try to coexist together peacefully.
7.	superpower	China will become a superpower in the twenty-first century.
8.	overpopulated	Many urban centers are overpopulated.
9.	postgraduate	Olga is doing postgraduate work at Cambridge University.

Pre-Reading (p. 129)

2.   1. c; 2. f; 3. a; 4. d; 5. g; 6. b; 7. e

Understanding the Reading (pp. 132–133)

1.   1. revelation; 2. perspicuity; 3. theories of inspiration; 4. canon; 5. inspiration; 6. dynamic theory; 7. inerrancy; 8. dictation theory; 9. illumination; 10. verbal theory; 11. infallibility

2. Answers may vary.

    1. Revelation is God's original communication of truth to humankind. Inspiration refers to the method God used to communicate and preserve the revelation of himself.

    2. Revelation is God's original communication of truth to humankind. Illumination is the internal working of the Holy Spirit to give understanding to the truth of God's Word.

    3. Illumination is the internal working of the Holy Spirit to give understanding to the truth of God's Word. Inspiration is the method God used to communicate and preserve the revelation of himself.

    4. Illumination is the internal working of the Holy Spirit to give understanding to the truth of God's Word. Perspicuity means that Scripture is sufficiently plain enough to be understood in all things necessary for salvation.

    5. Biblical infallibility refers to the trustworthiness of the Bible in matters of faith and practice. Biblical inerrancy refers to the idea that the Bible is completely free from error of any type.

    6. Historical authority refers to what God commanded within the historical setting in which the Bible was written. Normative authority refers to what is also binding upon us today that was binding upon those to whom God first spoke.

    7. The Roman Catholic view of the biblical canon accepts the Apocrypha as an equally authoritative part of the biblical canon as much as the Old and New Testaments. The Protestant view of the biblical canon has held that only the OT and NT books are the authoritative parts of Scripture.

Understanding Reading Skills and Grammar (p. 134)

1. c; 2. b; 3. d; 4. a; 5. g; 6. e; 7. f; 8. h

Reviewing Prefixes (pp. 134–136)

Answers may vary for rewritten items.

1. TRUE
2. FALSE: *Trial* does not contain a prefix. No part of the word can stand by itself.
3. TRUE
4. TRUE
5. FALSE: The word *bite* does not contain a prefix.
6. TRUE
7. TRUE
8. FALSE: *Mis-* means "wrongly" or "incorrectly."
9. TRUE
10. TRUE

11. TRUE
12. FALSE: *Ex-* means "formerly," "out of," or "from."
13. FALSE: The terms *premillennialism* and *postmillennialism* contain prefixes of time.
14. TRUE
15. TRUE
16. TRUE
17. FALSE: An illiterate person is someone who cannot read or write.

Reviewing Theological Vocabulary (pp. 136–137)

1. b; 2. b; 3. c; 4. b; 5. b; 6. a; 7. d; 8. b; 9. c

Evaluating Your Learning (p. 137)

Answers may vary.

Chapter 5

Word Forms (p. 140)

1. commitment, noun; 2. foundation, noun; 3. impose, verb; 4. precisely, adverb; 5. residence, noun; 6. predicted, verb

Vocabulary in Context (pp. 140–141)

1. c; 2. a; 3. b; 4. a; 5. c; 6. a

Word Definitions (pp. 141–142)

Answers may vary.
1. complex: complicated, intricate
2. adequate: acceptable, satisfactory
3. obvious: clear, apparent
4. foundational: principal, most basic, or underlying
5. resolve: settle, find a solution
6. elements: substances (atoms, etc.)
7. parallel: similarity (ideas side by side)
8. theme: idea, characteristic
9. predicted: stated before it happened, foretold
10. status: position, state

Word Families in Context (p. 142)

Paragraph 1: 1. human; 2. humankind; 3. humanity; 4. humanists
Paragraph 2: 1. sin; 2. sinned; 3. sinful; 4. sinners

Exercises (pp. 143–145)

1. 1. God is an infinite being.
    2. contrast between an infinite God and all other finite objects
    3. finite beings (objects) are bound by location and time; God is not limited by any of these
2. 1. The Christian church has had to combat heresy throughout history.
    2. heresy
    3. the debate over the Trinity; the debate over Jesus' humanity and deity
3. 1. the meaning of inerrancy in the Bible
    2. inerrancy
    3. the traditional meaning of inerrancy; the current understanding of inerrancy has become more complex and raises debate
4. main idea: a; sup. details: c, e; additional info: f
5. 1. a
    2. the people worshiped the Lord; their leaders gave instructions; people celebrated with great joy

Pre-Reading (pp. 145–146)

1. 1. ¶ 2; 2. ¶ 7; 3. ¶ 1; 4. ¶ 5; 5. ¶ 2; 6. ¶ 3
2. Answers may vary.
3. Answers may vary.
4. Adam and Eve in their initial, created, glorious state of innocence; humanity's fall into sin; humanity redeemed and renewed

Understanding the Reading (p. 149)

Answers may vary.

1. We belong to God who is our Creator and the one who has made us to be in a right relationship with himself. Human beings are distinct and different from all creatures. We are made for relationship with each other and the rest of creation. Every human being is valuable regardless of race, gender, age, or any other condition.
2. Since Adam and Eve lost their state of innocence, they fell from a condition of righteousness into a condition of sin both by nature and by action. Rejection of their relationship with God corrupted the image of God in which they were made. Thus, all human beings after them are sinners and share "solidarity with Adam in death."
3. God the Creator reveals himself as Redeemer by promising a Savior, Jesus Christ. Because Jesus stands before God in full and true humanity without sin, his salvific work, which was accomplished through his life, death, and resurrection, holds the possibility for sinful humanity to be restored to right relationship to himself.

Exercises (pp. 150–152)

1. 1. Some theorists have contended (that) humans are "pawns" of the underline. DO
    2. This concept undergirds (what) is said about human nature. DO
    3. The goal of the textual critic is to determine (which) variant is likely to be the closest. DO
    4. (That) we are made in God's image can also be explained in terms of relationships. S
    5. We are never told (what) the phrase means. DO
    6. "Now (what) you worship as something unknown I am going to proclaim to you." S
    7. (That) God is Creator is his basis for his right to rule the universe. S
    8. We must not forget (that) the origin of the soul is a mystery. DO
    9. The Bible is our essential source for understanding (what) sin is. DO
    10. (That) God keeps his promises is shown over and over again in Scripture. S
    11. "...(what) may be known is plain ..." (Rom 1:19) S
    12. The apparent universality of religions demonstrates (that) every human being has a type of knowledge of God. DO
    13. By "constitution" of human beings we mean (what) their makeup is or (how) they are composed. DO

2. 1. One of the debates between theologians is <u>how the basic constitution of human beings should be described</u>. SC
    2. Its foundational teaching is <u>that human beings are distinct and different from other creatures</u>. SC
    3. <u>Whatever view of human composition is employed</u>, it must acknowledge a creator. A
    4. Progressive revelation means <u>God initiated the revelation of himself</u>. – that
    5. The implication of 2 Tim 3:16 is <u>that God was directly involved in the written expression of revelation</u>. SC
    6. They can have varying points of view about <u>how God worked in the writing of the Bible</u>. OP
    7. Historic Christian belief is <u>that the process transpired under the Spirit and influence of God</u>. SC
    8. Physical death indicates <u>there is an end to life</u>. – that
    9. This gives us a significant degree of confidence in our knowledge of <u>what was originally written</u> OP
    10. God gives <u>whoever believes in his Son</u> eternal life. IO

3. 1. NC; 2. AC; 3. NC; 4. AC; 5. RAC; 6. AC; 7. NC; 8. RAC; 9. RAC; 10. AC; 11. AC; 12. NC; 13. NC; 14. AC; 15. AC; 16. NC; 17. NC; 18. AC; 19. NC; 20. RAC; 21. NC

Exercise (pp. 154–155)

1.	rejected	yes	eventual
2.	lived	yes	initial
3.		no	
4.	used	yes	interchangeable
5.		no	
6.	responsible	yes	full
7.		no	
8.		no	
9.	unable	yes	complete
10.	outline	yes	specific
11.		no	
12.	take	yes	literal
13.		no	
14.	tempted	yes	cunning

Exercises (pp. 156–157)

1. 1. d; 2. f; 3. a; 4. h; 5. i; 6. g; 7. c; 8. b; 9. j; 10. e
2. 1. sinless: without sin; 2. helpful: filled with help; 3. redemptive: characterized by redemption; 4. hasty: characterized by haste; 5. transcendent: have the quality of transcendence; 6. historical: pertaining to history; 7. continuous: quality of continuance; 8. changeable: able to change
3. 1. exists, eternally; 2. argument, logical; 3. Bible, historical; 4. comes, originally; 5. answer, obvious; 6. reveals, partially; 7. difference, significant; 8. aware, constantly; 9. understand, totally; 10. sinful, inherently

Pre-Reading (p. 157)

1. The Constitutional Nature of Human Persons, The Transmission of Sin
2. dichotomism, trichotomism, monism
3. Pelagianism or Semi-Pelagianism, realism or natural headship

Understanding the Reading (pp. 160–161)

Answers may vary.

1. The passage sets up a contrast between Adam and Jesus Christ. Adam brought sin and death while Christ brings righteousness and life.
2. Romans 12:12–19 states that sin entered into the world through Adam and death through sin; thus all sinned. Pelagius believed that Adam's sin injured only himself and is simply a bad example for humankind. There was no transmission of sin to his offspring.
3. Semi-Pelagianism asserts that transmission of sin is passed to another like a disease. Humans are sick and need the aid of a Great Physician. Pelagius did not believe in the transmission of sin.

4. The school of realism interprets Romans 5:12 literally. All genetic humanity existed in the person of Adam. His sin was the sin of the whole human race.

5. Federal headship is the view that humans inherit their physical natures from their parents but their souls were created by God and united with the body at the appropriate time. The connection with Adam means that we were represented by him.

6. It is essential that we admit that we are sinners in need of forgiveness. We must turn to Jesus Christ who is our righteousness and live in the new life given to us in Him.

Pre-Reading (p. 161)

2.   a.   pre-existence of the soul, traducianism, creationism.

  b.   literal view, mythical view, historical view.

  c.   Total depravity does not mean that human beings are as sinful as they can possibly be, that human beings engage in every kind of sin, or that human beings are incapable of doing anything that is good or lack conscience regarding right and wrong.

Understanding the Reading (p. 164)

1. e; 2. g; 3. j; 4. c; 5. i; 6. l; 7. k; 8. a; 9. f; 10. b; 11. h; 12. d

Reviewing Noun Clauses (pp. 164–165)

1. The good news is (that) God has been at work to restore his creation to its intended purpose.

2. People have different ideas about (why) things happen, (why) they are the way they are, (what) the proper goals are.

3. (What) Jesus thought and believed about himself demonstrates his unique nature.

4. He tells us (what) he wants us to know. He tells us (who) he is, (what) he has done, (what) he is doing, and (what) he will do. He also tells us (what) he requires of us.

5. Since the term *total depravity* is often misunderstood, it is helpful to clarify (what) it does *not* mean. It does not mean (that) human beings are as sinful as they can possibly be; it does not mean (that) they engage in every possible form of sin; nor does it mean (that) we are incapable of doing anything good or (that) we lack conscience regarding right and wrong. Total depravity does mean (that) sin has affected the very core of the person. It means also (that) all areas or aspects of our nature are affected by sin.

Reviewing Suffixes (p. 165)

Answers may vary for rewritten items.

1. FALSE: Inflectional suffixes never change the meaning of a word.

2. TRUE

3. TRUE

4. FALSE: Not every word ending in *-ly* is an adverb.

5. TRUE
6. FALSE: Derivational suffixes change a word's meaning.
7. TRUE
8. TRUE
9. TRUE
10. FALSE: Although family ends in -ly, it is not an adverb; it is a noun.

Reviewing Theological Vocabulary (pp. 166–167)
1. b; 2. c; 3. d; 4. b; 5. d; 6. c; 7. a; 8. b; 9. b; 10. b

Evaluating Your Learning (p. 167)
Answers may vary.

Chapter 6

Vocabulary in Context (pp. 170–171)
1. c; 2. c; 3. b; 4. b; 5. c; 6. a

Word Forms in Context (pp. 171–172)
Answers may vary.

1a.	noun	The focus of his sermon was on the person of Jesus Christ.
1b.	verb	His sermon focuses on Christ's humanity.
2a.	verb	She substituted spinach for broccoli in the recipe.
2b.	noun	We had a substitute in our French class.
3a.	verb	He stresses the important points in his paper.
3b.	noun	The manager was under a lot of stress to meet the production deadline.
4a.	verb	Educators believe that parental involvement in their children's education is linked to better performance in school.
4b.	noun	The researchers found a link between smoking and lung cancer.
5a.	noun	There are various social functions at the community center on weekends.
5b.	verb	His old car functioned poorly.

Dictionary Use (pp. 172–173)
Answers may vary.
1. behalf: in the interest of
2. equip: to prepare for a particular task
3. expand: to make larger, more extensive
4. hence: for this reason
5. normal: usual or typical

6.   previous: occurring before in time

7.   similar: having a resemblance in appearance or character

8.   technical: a word relating to a particular subject

Word Families in Context (p. 173)

Paragraph 1: 1. ascending; 2. ascension; 3. ascended; 4. ascend

Paragraph 2: 1. sacrifices; 2. sacrifice; 3. sacrificial; 4. sacrificially

Exercises (pp. 174–175)

1.   1.   Evidence about the unique origin of Jesus from the four Gospels.

       2.   Matthew and Luke affirm that he was born of a woman who had not
             had sexual relations with a man (i.e., virgin birth). Mark introduces
             Jesus as the Son of God and the bearer of the kingdom of God. John
             declares Jesus to be the "Word," who existed before and took part in
             the creation of the world.

2.   1.   Jesus is fully human as well as divine.

       2.   The Gospels not only provide ample evidences of Jesus' full deity but
             also his full humanity.

       3.   His ancestry, which points to his human descent, is traced in both
             Matthew and Luke. He was born the way other babies are born and
             grew according to normal growth and development patterns within
             the confines of a human family (Lk 2:39–40, 52).

3.   1.   The word *ransom* as metaphor describing the saving work of Christ.

       2.   This word carries the idea of paying a price in order to reclaim that
             which one previously possessed.

Pre-Reading (p. 175)

1.   Answers may vary.

2.   Answers may vary.

3.   Messiah, Son of Man, Suffering Servant

Understanding the Reading (p. 178)

1.   Although Jesus accepted the messianic designation, he redefined it and
      linked it with other titles: "the Son of Man" and "the Servant" who would
      suffer.

2.   The Son of Man (Dan 7:13–14) is a heavenly, spiritual person whose concern
      was for all humankind. When Jesus used this term, he identified himself as
      this heavenly figure, thus showing that the term *Son of Man* refers to his
      deity.

3.   As Messiah, Jesus was anointed to carry out and fulfill God's plan of salvation
      and restoration. As Son of Man, he had the highest position of all. As
      Servant, he suffered so that others might be saved.

4.   Answers may vary. Matthew and Luke point to his ancestry which refers to
      his human descent. Luke 2:30–40, 52 talks about his birth and growth as a

boy in a human family. Jesus was limited by physical factors such as hunger, and weariness. Jesus suffered physically and died (Jn 19:33–34) yet with all this he never sinned.

5.   Answers may vary. It is important to understand Jesus' deity and humanity because there is a great gap between sinful man and a holy God. The incarnation in which deity and humanity are united in one person makes the bridging of this gap possible. Jesus, fully man and fully God, became man for the work of redemption.

Pre-Reading (p. 178)

1.   Was Jesus truly God? Was Jesus truly human? How can God and man be united in one person?

2.   divinity and humanity

Understanding the Reading (pp. 180–181)

1.   Jesus is truly God. Christians worship him and since only God can be worshiped it would be idolatrous if he is not God. Jesus Christ shows us what God is like because he is God. Finally, he overcomes the forces of sin and death and only God can do that. Only God, the Creator, can change history, defeat Satan and death, and restore creation—this is the work of Christ.

2.   The four Gospels show that Jesus is fully man, and thus the divine truth of his full humanity must be accepted.

3.   According to the Council of Chalcedon, Christ had two natures united in one person. He was fully God and fully man. The union of two natures occurs without confusion, change, division, or separation. The Scriptures witness that Jesus is the man in whom we encounter God himself.

4.   perfect in humanness; actually man, with a rational soul and a body; same reality as we are ourselves as far as our humanness; like us in all respects, sin only excepted; born of Mary the virgin; God-bearer in respect to his humanness

5.   perfect in deity; actually God; the same reality as God as far as his deity; before time began, begotten of the Father; one and only Christ; Lord; Logos of God, the Lord Jesus Christ

6.   Answers may vary.

Exercise (pp. 182–183)

Answers may vary.

1.	to make regular	He takes medication to regulate his diabetes.
2.	to make dark	The clouds darken the sky.
3.	to make final	I will finalize my decision on the contract next week.
4.	to make light	I will lighten your load by carrying those books.
5.	to make a category	She will categorize the different files today.
6.	to make simple	Can you simplify your request?
7.	to make clear	Please clarify what you want me to do.

8.　to set free　　　　　He will liberate the prisoners.

Exercises (pp. 184–186)

1.　1.　believ er　　　believe　　　someone who believes
　　2.　fulfill ment　　fulfill　　　something which fulfills
　　3.　modern ist　　modern　　　someone who values modern ideas
　　4.　persist ence　　persist　　　the quality to continue
　　5.　righteous ness　righteous　　the quality of being righteous
　　6.　human ity　　　human　　　the state of being human
　　7.　adopt ion　　　adopt　　　the act of adopting
　　8.　creat or　　　create　　　the one who creates
　　9.　inerr ancy　　inerrant　　the quality of being without error
　　10.　interpret ation　interpret　　the act of interpreting
　　11.　Egypt ian　　Egypt　　　someone from Egypt
　　12.　Israel ite　　Israel　　　someone from Israel

2.　1.　the study of man/humanity
　　2.　the study of Christ
　　3.　the study of salvation
　　4.　the study of the church
　　5.　the study of last things

3.　1.　materialism　　the idea that the highest values lie in material well-being
　　　　materialist　　someone who values things / material well-being
　　2.　idealism　　the practice of forming ideals or living under their influence
　　　　idealist　　one who believes in idealism
　　3.　deism　　belief which denies the Creator's influence with the laws of nature
　　　　deist　　someone who believes in deism
　　4.　legalism　　strict conformity to religious creed
　　　　legalist　　one who lives in strict conformity to religious creed
　　5.　theism　　belief in the existence of God
　　　　theist　　one who believes in the existence of God
　　6.　dispensationalism　a particular teaching regarding the way God deals with humanity
　　　　dispensationalist　one who holds to the teaching of dispensationalism
　　7.　animism　　belief in the existence of spirits separate from bodies
　　　　animist　　one who believes in the existence of spirits
　　8.　modernism　　set of beliefs that value contemporary ideas
　　　　modernist　　someone who holds to contemporary ideas

9.	pragmatism	the idea that truth is to be tested by the practical outcomes of belief
	pragmatist	someone who holds to pragmatic ideas
10.	atheism	the teaching that there is no God
	atheist	someone who holds to the teaching of atheism

Pre-Reading (p. 186)

Answers may vary.

Understanding the Reading (p. 189)

Answers may vary.

1. The overarching characteristic of Jesus' work was to obey his Father's will. (See Jn 4:34.)

2. Some of the activities that Jesus did to carry out his Father's will were: preaching and teaching; announcing, clarifying, and establishing the kingdom of God on earth; calling people to follow him; healing the sick; casting out demons; stilling the storm; feeding the 5000; raising the dead; dying on the cross; rising from the dead; ascending to the Father; and commissioning others to proclaim him to the world. These activities were important for establishing in a new way the rule and reign of God on earth. (See ¶ 3.)

3. The atonement is necessary because Christ provided the means for a holy God and sinful humanity to be reconciled.

4. The New Testament portrays Christ's work of reconciliation through substitution (Christ took upon himself the consequence of sin—being separated from God), ransom (Jesus is the ransom provided by God through his death so that humanity can be redeemed), and sacrifice (Jesus is the once-for-all sacrifice for our sins). The significance and powerful implications of the atonement are beyond us but these different portrayals help us to understand in a limited way just what Christ did for us.

Pre-Reading (p. 190)

Prophet, Priest, King

Understanding the Reading (p. 191)

1. Answers may vary.

   a. prophet: Jesus, the "second Moses" was the fulfillment of Moses' words, "The Lord your God will raise up for you a prophet like me from among your own brothers. You must listen to him" (Deut 34:10–11). Jesus is God's representative to his people; he is the end of the prophetic line.

   b. priest: Jesus is described in Hebrews 4:14–5:6 as our "great high priest" who is the representative of and intercedes for his people before God. Jesus is the end of the priestly line.

c.   king: David was the great king over the Hebrew people. Jesus, the Son of David and also the Son of Man, rules over all peoples, nations, and languages, and his kingdom is everlasting (Dan 7:13–14). He is the King of kings.

Pre-Reading (p. 192)

1.   Answers may vary. Christology is the theological study of the person and work of Jesus Christ.

2.   Ransom Theory, Moral-Influence Theory, Satisfaction Theory

3.   Answers may vary.

Understanding the Reading (pp. 197–198)

1.   1. P; 2. P; 3. W; 4. P; 5. W; 6. W; 7. W; 8. P; 9. X; 10. P; 11. W; 12. P; 13. P; 14. W; 15. X; 16. P

2.   1. incarnation; 2. ransom; 3. state of humiliation of Christ; 4. substitution; 5. parousia; 6. state of exaltation of Christ

3.   1. sacrifice; 2. homoiousios; 3. ascension; 4. expiation; 5. parousia; 6. homoousios; 7. ransom; 8. propitiation

Reviewing Suffixes (p. 198)

Words with multiple suffixes

1.	faith <u>fulness</u>	faith
2.	Calvin <u>istic</u>	Calvin
3.	concept <u>ualize</u>	concept
4.	simpl <u>ification</u>	simple
5.	Christ <u>ianity</u>	Christ
6.	incarnat <u>ional</u>	incarnate
7.	theolog <u>ically</u>	theology
8.	execut <u>ioner</u>	execute
9.	sacrific <u>ially</u>	sacrifice

Reviewing Prefixes and Suffixes (p. 199)

Words with prefixes and suffixes

1.	bibl <u>ical</u>	adjective
2.	human <u>ity</u>	noun
3.	ful <u>ly</u>	adverb
4.	class <u>ify</u>	verb
5.	judg <u>ment</u>	noun
6.	educat <u>ion</u>	noun
7.	hope <u>lessness</u>	noun
8.	nation <u>alistic</u>	adjective
9.	margin <u>alize</u>	verb

10.	histor <u>ically</u>	adverb
11.	<u>pre</u>-public <u>ation</u>	noun
12.	<u>un</u>faith <u>ful</u>	adjective
13.	infallibil <u>ity</u>	noun
14.	<u>over</u>simpl <u>ify</u>	verb
15.	<u>inter</u>change <u>ably</u>	adverb
16.	mono<u>ton</u> <u>ous</u>	adjective
17.	nonjudg <u>mental</u>	adjective
18.	<u>re</u>activ <u>ate</u>	verb
19.	inerr <u>ancy</u>	noun
20.	<u>dis</u>honest <u>ly</u>	adverb
21.	<u>under</u>state <u>ment</u>	noun

Reviewing Theological Vocabulary (pp. 199–200)

1. d; 2. a; 3. b; 4. c; 5. d; 6. c; 7. a; 8. c; 9. b; 10. b

Evaluating Your Learning (pp. 200–201)

Answers may vary.

Chapter 7

Word Forms (p. 204)

1. community, noun; 2. comprehensive, adjective; 3. legal, adjective; 4. sections, noun; 5. symbol, noun

Word Definitions (p. 205)

Answers may vary.

1. instructed: commanded
2. confirm: establish the truth or correctness
3. context: consideration of the surrounding words or principles
4. quotes: repeats
5. acquires: obtains
6. reacting: responding in a certain way
7. proceeds: comes forth
8. contributing: helping to cause or bring about
9. accompaniment: something that supports or adds to the experience
10. transform: make a dramatic change in

Dictionary Use (pp. 205–206)

Answers may vary.

1. denote: to indicate, to be a sign of

2. furthermore: in addition, also
3. principal: main, important
4. section: a distinct portion

Word Families in Context (p. 206)

Paragraph 1: 1. calls; 2. calling; 3. called; 4. call

Paragraph 2: 1. revived; 2. revival; 3. revivalism; 4. revivalist; 5. revivals

Exercises (pp. 206–207)

1. 1. c; 2. a
2. 1. an explanation of the biblical concept of conversion
   2. Whereas regeneration is seen as the beginning of new life in Jesus Christ from God's perspective, conversion is the beginning of the Christian life from the human perspective.

Exercise (pp. 208–209)

1. marker: on the other hand
   comparison/contrast: inflectional suffixes – derivational suffixes
2. marker: Although
   comparison/contrast: modify verbs – describe adjectives
3. marker: like
   comparison/contrast: human beings + Jesus
4. marker: while
   comparison/contrast: "Son of Man" – "Son of God"
5. marker: both . . . and
   comparison/contrast: universal church + individual congregations
6. marker: similar to
   comparison/contrast: subordinationism + previously held view
7. marker: instead
   comparison/contrast: distinctiveness of each nature – "properties" of each nature
8. marker: like
   comparison/contrast: a sound + a mighty wind
9. marker: yet
   comparison/contrast: The conflict continues and is severe – Satan is never able to carry out his activity
10. marker: However
    comparison/contrast: come from the Old Testament – OT meaning is reinterpreted, developed, or expanded
11. marker: neither . . . nor; deceiving + being deceived
12. marker: in contrast to; the God of Israel – the false claimants to deity
13. marker: neither
    comparison/contrast: my thoughts are not your thoughts – my ways are not your ways

marker: as . . . so
comparison/contrast: the heavens are higher than the earth + my ways are higher than your ways and my thoughts are higher than your thoughts

14. marker: even though
comparison/contrast: semi-Pelagians disagreed – it was argued
marker: like
comparison/contrast: transmission of sin + disease

15. marker: just as . . . so
comparison/contrast: God breathed breath of life into humankind + Scriptures divinely produced
marker: similarly
comparison/contrast: God the Holy Spirit is the primary author + human beings are secondary authors

16. marker: similiar to
comparison/contrast: the physical nature or body + plants and animals
marker: but
comparison/contrast: similiar in kind – different in degree of complexity

Exercise (pp. 211–212)

1. marker: in order to
cause: to use and further extend the moral and spiritual faculties they already have
effect/result: to make progress toward attaining God-likeness

2. marker: resulted in
cause: The supernatural influence of the Holy Spirit upon the biblical writers
effect/result: an accurate record of self-revelation

3. marker: because
cause: He is already perfect
effect/result: God's nature does not change

4. marker: as a result of
cause: his will and actions
effect/result: all things have come into being

5. marker: as a result
cause: Cyrus, King of Persia, issued a decree permitting the return of the Hebrew captives to their homeland
effect/result: the temple in Jerusalem was rebuilt

6. marker: because
cause: they understood the words that had been read to them
effect/result: all the people went away and celebrated with great joy

7. marker: in order to

   cause: the reader must become familiar with the background of the written text

   effect/result: understand what the author intended

8. marker: stem from

   cause: influences of a writer's worldview

   effect/result: questioning or rejecting biblical authority

9. marker: so that

   cause: Mark out a straight path for your feet

   effect/result: those who are weak and lame will not fall

10. marker: as a result

    cause: those who do hold to the inspiration of Scripture can have varying points of view about how God worked in its production

    effect/result: numerous theories have been formulated

11. marker: since

    cause: our knowledge of God comes through the Bible

    effect/result: we place ourselves under the authority of the Bible

12. marker: due to

    cause: our finiteness and fallenness

    effect/result: we cannot know God unless he reveals himself to us

13. marker: so that

    cause: God had to speak

    effect/result: he could know God's will

14. marker: lead to

    cause: overemphasize the immanence of God

    result/effect: a form of pantheism, meaning "everything is God"

15. marker: consequently

    cause: prone to go our own self-centered way

    effect/result: we need more than the knowledge we gain through nature

16. marker: in order to

    cause: our overall approach should be to enter the world of the Bible and live there

    effect/result: understand a passage in the context in which it was written

    effect/result: interpret it

    effect/result: apply the truths to our own context

17. markers: because, because, because

    cause: we believe that he is our Father who is in heaven

    cause: we believe that he is our Saviour, Jesus Christ, the Son

    cause: we believe that he is the Holy Spirit who is present within the believer

    effect/result: why we worship God as a triune God

18. markers: since, since

    cause: the writers of the Bible were selected by God and in various ways received their information from him

    cause: many were indeed eyewitnesses and participants in that which they described

    effect/result: we may place full confidence in what they have written

19. marker: because of

    cause: human finiteness and human limitations

    effect/result: illumination of the Holy Spirit is needed

    marker: result from

    cause: human sinfulness

    effect/result: human finiteness and human limitations

Pre-Reading (p. 213)

1. Answers may vary.
2. Answers may vary.
3. omnipresence, omniscience, omnipotence

Understanding the Reading (pp. 215–216)

1. Some of the evidence is: (1) Jesus understood the Holy Spirit to be one who possesses the qualities of a person. When referring to the Holy Spirit (*pneuma*), Jesus uses the masculine form of the pronoun rather than the neuter form. (2) Luke relates an incident where the Holy Spirit speaks to a group in worship, telling them to "set aside Barnabas and Saul . . ." (Acts 13:2). (3) The Holy Spirit exercises qualities of a person such as understanding, wisdom, counsel, knowledge, and power. (4) The Holy Spirit is referred to in Scripture as our teacher, guide, comforter, one who sanctifies. He also reproves, speaks, empowers, and brings about salvation. He has feelings such as grief. He can be loved, obeyed, reverenced, etc.

2. Jesus described the Holy Spirit as one who possesses the qualities of a person. By using the masculine form of the pronoun with the neuter noun *pneuma*, this shows that Jesus viewed him as a person. Jesus referred to him as "another of the same kind," or one who is identified closely with himself.

3. Evidence that the Holy Spirit is divine is: (1) the term *holy* ascribes to his being God. He is the cause of holiness in human beings. (2) He possesses divine attributes (omniscience, omnipresence, omnipotence) which only God possesses. (3) In the Old Testament whatever is said of the Lord (Jehovah) is also said of the Spirit of the Lord. (4) In the New Testament the interchangeable language such as "The Holy Spirit spoke the truth to your forefathers when he said through Isaiah the prophet..." (Acts 28:25–26). Phrases that speak of the indwelling Spirit of Christ and the Spirit of God refer to the life-giving Holy Spirit that dwells in the believer. (5) The trinitarian passages in the New Testament connote equality of the three persons. The word *name* is singular, signifying unity of these three persons.

Pre-Reading (p. 216)

1. to give the message of God to prophets, to grant skills for various tasks, and to raise up leadership to serve the people of Israel.
2. Answers may vary.
3. Answers may vary.

Understanding the Reading (p. 219)

1. The OT gives evidence of the Holy Spirit at work in creation, giving a message of God to the prophets (such as Ezekiel), granting skills for tasks (such as constructing the tabernacle), and raising up leadership for the people of Israel (such as Moses and David).
2. The NT gives evidence of the Holy Spirit at work in the incarnation, Jesus' life, his baptism, his time in the desert to face the enemy, and his power to teach in the synagogues, preach to the multitudes, do miracles, and drive out demons. After his ascension to the Father, Jesus' presence with the disciples was through the Holy Spirit.
3. Answers may vary.

Pre-Reading (p. 219)

1. ¶ 7; 2. ¶ 8, 3. ¶ 5

Understanding the Reading (pp. 221–222)

1. in the Holy Spirit and the written Scriptures working together
2. The controversy stems from the addition by the Western church of the phrase "proceeding from the Father and from the Son" which the Eastern Greek church rejected.
3. The impact is emphasis on the Holy Spirit and the special manifestations or gifts of the Holy Spirit.
4. Answers may vary.

Pre-Reading (p. 222)

1. Answers may vary.
2. a. John 3:5 and Titus 3:5
   b. Rom 12:6–8, 1 Cor 12–14, Eph 4:7–13, 1 Pet 4:10–11

Understanding the Reading (pp. 226–227)

1. 1. fruit of the Spirit; 2. Paraclete; 3. glossolalia; 4. common grace; 5. subordinationism; 6. regeneration; 7. special grace; 8. conversion; 9. revivalism
2. 1. Common grace is associated with the work of the Holy Spirit in nature and human life. Special grace refers to the work of the Holy Spirit to effect change within the human heart.
   2. Regeneration is the biblical teaching that emphasizes the new birth of fallen human beings by the indwelling of the Holy Spirit. Baptismal

regeneration is the view (from the Roman Catholic and other groups with that perspective) that baptism confers grace upon the individual, washing away original sin.

3. Life in the flesh is characterized by bondage to one's human nature and is concerned with self. Life in the Spirit is characterized by submission to the Spirit of God and is concerned with the glory of God.

4. General (external) calling comes to all who hear the Word of God and the gospel and are invited to accept Christ in repentance and faith. Effective (internal) calling means that the external calling that has been heard is made effective in the heart of the sinner through the work of the Holy Spirit.

5. Regeneration emphasizes the new birth of fallen human beings by the indwelling of the Holy Spirit. Conversion refers to real repentance and faith of an individual in the person of Christ and his work, resulting in salvation.

6. Gifts of the Spirit are spiritual gifts given to believers for the purpose of edification of and service to the church. Fruit of the Spirit are positive virtues (e.g., love, joy, peace) that are evidence of the indwelling Holy Spirit.

Reviewing Theological Vocabulary (pp. 227–228)

Answers may vary for rewritten items.

1. FALSE: This teaching believes that the Holy Spirit has an inferior nature, role, and status within the Trinity.
2. TRUE
3. FALSE: They rejected the authority of the church leaders and sought only the direct guidance of the Holy Spirit.
4. TRUE
5. TRUE
6. FALSE: Conversion is the beginning of new life in Christ from the human perspective.
7. TRUE
8. TRUE
9. FALSE: Life in the flesh is characterized by bondage to one's human nature.
10. TRUE

Reviewing Organizational Markers (pp. 228–229)

1. As a consequence (C); 2. Even though (U); 3. stems from (C); 4. although (U); 5. like (L); 6. because (C); 7. just as (L); 8. yet (U); 9. similarly (L); 10. contribute to (C); 11. as a result (C); 12. neither . . . nor, neither . . . nor, neither . . . nor, nor, neither . . . nor, nor (L); 13. At the same time (U); 14. hence (C); 15. on the other hand (U)

Evaluating Your Learning (p. 229)

Answers may vary.

Chapter 8

Word Forms (p. 233)

1. considered; 2. mutual; 3. purchased; 4. security; 5. successor

Vocabulary in Context (pp. 233–234)

1. b; 2. c; 3. a; 4. d; 5. d; 6. c

Dictionary Use (p. 234)

Answers may vary.

1. access: a means of approaching, the right to enter
2. appreciate: to understand, to recognize the worth of, to be fully aware of
3. conduct: the way one acts, behavior
4. crucial: critical, of supreme importance
5. intrinsic: essential, inherent
6. prior: previous, earlier
7. relevant: pertinent, relating to
8. whereas: although, while

Word Families in Context (p. 235)

Paragraph 1: 1. saving; 2. saved; 3. salvation; 4. save
Paragraph 2: 1. identification; 2. identified; 3. identify; 4. identity

Word Definitions (pp. 235–236)

Answers may vary.

1.	everyday	rescuing a life, preserving
	theological	delivering from sin's power
2.	everyday	something changed from one use to another
	theological	individual's turning from sin and turning to God by accepting the work of Christ Jesus on one's behalf
3.	everyday	the process of buying back something
	theological	the process by which a ransom is paid through the death of Jesus Christ in order to redeem human beings from the bondage of sin
4.	everyday	something that is beautiful or worthy of praise
	theological	the time when believers are fully conformed to the image and likeness of Jesus Christ
5.	everyday	the act of being vindicated as in a court case
	theological	God transfers the righteousness of Christ to the believer and considers that person "not guilty"

6. everyday   to clear up something; to make up for a wrong done
   theological   to justify the guilty sinner

7. everyday   something new like a line of clothing or an original work of art
   theological   the complete change that happens to someone who is
                   reconciled with God

Exercises (pp. 236–237)

1. 1. definition of forgiveness
   2. In Acts 13:38 Paul associates forgiveness with salvation. Christ's forgiveness means that the sin has been both pardoned and cleansed and the sinner is now guiltless in God's eyes (1 Cor 1:8). Since believers are still subject to sin after conversion, they must continue to repent of sin and ask God's forgiveness.

2. 1. The Scriptures attribute salvation to God.
   2. the OT words associated with the idea of salvation; the NT gives the fullest revelation of salvation
   3. OT meaning: deliverance by Yahweh from danger of many types; NT meaning: The work of Christ is applied to human lives.

3. 1. how the term righteousness is used
   2. may refer to what God requires; refers to the status of the sinner pronounced not guilty by God
   3. God transfers the righteousness of Christ to the believer. This is what is meant by justification.

Pre-Reading (p. 238)

1. Answers may vary. The worldview of the biblical writers covers the span of human history and more. It shows us salvation in the context of God's larger plan to bring about the complete restoration and victory through Jesus Christ.

2. Answers may vary. The chart or drawing should include these four phases: creation, the fall, the process of redemption and restoration, and the consummation.

Understanding the Reading (p. 240)

1. Answers may vary. The doctrine of salvation is essential for understanding God's nature and actions. By understanding the depth of his plan through Jesus Christ, we can better communicate this message to others.

2. The Old Testament words associated with the idea of salvation speak of deliverance by Yahweh from danger of many types, help in distress, and setting free and healing. God's people of the OT looked at salvation as a real and present experience based on this. For example, Abraham believed God and his faith was credited to him for righteousness (Gen 15:6), God rescued Abraham's descendants from Egypt in the exodus (Ex 20), and God led the Israelites through priests, judges, kings, and prophets. (Answers may vary for the last part of the question.)

3. a. In the "first exodus," God delivered His people from 400 years of bondage in Egypt through his servant Moses. On the other hand, the "second exodus," which refers to deliverance from the slavery of sin and death, is grounded in the life, ministry, teaching, death, and resurrection of Jesus Christ (Rom 6:6).

    b. The first Passover was observed just before the Israelites were about to leave Egypt and it was a picture of Jesus' sacrificial death. Jesus' observance of the Passover with his disciples gave it new meaning. The writer of Hebrews demonstrates that Jesus Christ has once and for all accomplished all that Moses, Joshua, the Old Testament priests, and the form of worship foreshadowed and symbolized.

4. Answers may vary. Example: With sensitivity it would be important to focus on passages such as Acts 4:12 that says, "Salvation is found in no one else, for there is no other name under heaven given to men by which we must be saved." This is not a popular message today in our tolerant world but this is the way God has provided for those who would believe.

Pre-Reading (p. 241)

1. 1. A, B; 2. A; 3. A, B; 4. A, B; 5. A, B; 6. A, B; 7. neither; 8. A

2. Entry word: Salvation
    Word in original language(s): Hebrew root *yāšā;* Greek term *sōtēria*
    Definition: Redemption from the power and effects of sin
    Biblical reference: Acts 7:25; 27:31; Heb. 11:7; Rom. 5:1–11, etc.
    Cross-Reference: See also Savior
    Abbreviations: Heb. Rom. Eph. Phil., etc.
    Bibliography: none
    Authorship: R.E.O. White

Understanding the Reading (pp. 242–243)

1. by what we are saved from; by noting that salvation is past; by distinguishing salvation's various aspects

2. Sin and death; guilt and estrangement; ignorance of truth; bondage to vices; fear of demons, of death, of life, of God, of hell.

3. Answers may vary. Example: Paul's testimony shows how salvation brings peace with God, access to his favor, endurance in suffering for the sake of the gospel, etc.

4. Salvation includes that which was given freely by God's grace in the new birth (past); that which is continually imparted in terms of sanctification (present); and the enjoyment of eternal life and that which is still to be attained, which is the redemption of the body and final glory (future).

5. 1. religious   acceptance with God, forgiveness, reconciliation

    2. emotional   peace, courage, hopefulness

    3. practical   prayer, guidance, discipline, dedication, service

    4. ethical   new moral dynamic for new moral aims, freedom, victory

    5. personal   new thoughts, convictions, motives

6.　social　　new sense of community with Christians, of compassion toward all, overriding impulse to love as Jesus loved

Pre-Reading (p. 243)

1. Old Testament, New Testament, Relationship to non-biblical views, Biblical summary
2. Atonement, Forgiveness, Justification, Reconciliation, Redemption

Understanding the Reading (pp. 245–246)

1. It means 'bring to a spacious environment' with a metaphorical sense of being freed from limitation. Two examples are deliverance from disease (Is. 38:20) or trouble (Je. 30:7).
2. Gnosticism　　claimed special knowledge of God; intellectual over moral; the soul's escape from the domination of physical passions and astrological forces

   Mystery Religions from fate; achieved by cultic rituals; non-moral; no great saving acts

   NT Writers　　moral and spiritual deliverance; God's free gift to those who trust the righteousness of Christ; both a present reality and a future promise
3. Answers may vary. (1) It is historical because God has worked within the context of history. (2) It is moral and spiritual by delivering people from sin and guilt, not necessarily physical hardships. (3) It is eschatological in that it relates to the future complete establishment of God's kingdom.

Exercises (pp. 247–248)

1. 1. in credible: to believe; 2. anthropology: human; 3. cosmos: world, universe; 4. corporal: body; 5. gender: kind; 6. crucify: to fasten, to torture; 7. crucial: to fasten, to torture; 8. miniature: little, less; 9. cosmology: world, universe; 10. generations: birth, kind
2. 1. incredulous; 2. cosmopolitan; 3. minimal; 4. microcosm; 5. discreditable; 6. anthropology; 7. regeneration; 8. corporation; 9. crux; 10. congenital

Exercises (pp. 249–250)

1. 1. per mitted: to send, to let go; 2. sym pathy: feeling, suffering; 3. im mortality: death; 4. inter rupts: to break, to burst; 5. trans mit: to send, to let go; 6. dis rupted: to break, to burst; 7. reign: rule, right, direct; 8. a pathy: feeling, suffering; 9. mortify: death; 10. omni potent: powerful
2. 1. philosophy; 2. mortality; 3. commit; 4. sovereignty; 5. potential; 6. permit; 7. missile; 8. abrupt; 9. pathetic; 10. mortification

Exercises (pp. 250–251)

1. 1. omni science: to know or discern; 2. theology: God; 3. in vincible: to conquer, to show conclusively; 4. sanctuary: sacred, holy; 5. re viving: live,

alive; 6. victorious: to conquer, to show conclusively; 7. a typical: impression, image, likeness; 8. sanctions: sacred, holy

2.   1. survive; 2. convict; 3. sanctify; 4. typology; 5. theocentric; 6. theophany; 7. unscientific; 8. sanctity

3.   1. sove reign; 2. sub mit; 3. im mortality or im mortality; 4. mortal or mortal; 5. incor ruptible; 6. con vincing; 7. con victing; 8. re generation; 9. com mit; 10. sanctification

Pre-Reading (p. 252)

1.   Answers may vary.
2.   the Bible, prayer, worship, fellowship, witness, service, and the Holy Spirit
3.   Answers may vary.

Understanding the Reading (p. 254)

Answers may vary.

1.   God the Father gave us salvation through the work and person of Jesus Christ. Therefore, the new life of the believer is ordered and planned by God the Father.
2.   God the Son purchased our salvation and we are to become like him. Christ is the Head of the church.
3.   God the Holy Spirit is the one who applies, seals, and directs our new life. He sanctifies, fills, dominates, controls, guides, chastens, and empowers believers and the church to grow into maturity of Christ.

Pre-Reading (p. 255)

1.   The article is about what it means to be identified with Christ.
2.   vine and branch, hand and body, marriage relationship (Christ and the church)
3.   Answers may vary.

Understanding the Reading (pp. 256–257)

Answers may vary. Examples:

1.   Being "in Christ" is accomplished by the baptism of the Holy Spirit, a divine act of grace and power. The position of being "in Christ" is described with many pictures, including the vine and the branches, the head and the body, and the marriage relationship.
2.   These readings have helped me by explaining (1) the resources given to the believer for growth and maturity, (2) the role of the Holy Spirit in spiritual growth, and (3) what it means to have the position of being "in Christ."

Pre-Reading (p. 257)

1.   Answers may vary. Examples:
     adoption: the part of salvation in which God makes the sinner his child
     justification: a legal term that means "to declare righteous"

sanctification: the believer is set apart, made holy, and dedicated to God

antinomianism: an erroneous view which holds that God's grace removes one's obligation to the moral law of the Old Testament

legalism: the attitude which equates morality and spirituality with strict obedience to a set of laws

2.   Terms from Daily Life
1. physical birth and life; 2. family relationships; 3. personal relationships; 4. religious ceremony; 5. court of law; 6. commerce

Temporal Aspects of Salvation
1. predestination; 2. effectual calling; 3. grace; 4. regeneration; 5. conversion; 6. repentance; 7. faith; 8. forgiveness; 9. union with Christ; 10. eternal life; 11. sanctification; 12. perseverance; 13. hope; 14. glorification

Understanding the Reading (pp. 264–265)

1. antinomianism; 2. free will; 3. glorification; 4. common grace; 5. sanctification; 6. imputation; 7. predestination; 8. adoption; 9. prevenient grace; 10. regeneration; 11. propitiation; 12. legalism; 13. special grace; 14. reconciliation; 15. justification; 16. irresistible grace; 17. conversion

Reviewing Theological Vocabulary (pp. 265–266)

1. b; 2. d; 3. b; 4. a; 5. d; 6. b; 7. c; 8. a; 9. b; 10. c; 11. a; 12. c; 13. b; 14. a

Reviewing Roots (p. 266)

1. crucify: to fasten, to torture; 2. cosmos: world, universe, order; 3. em pathy: feeling, suffering; 4. sove reign: rule, right, direct; 5. cor rupted: to break, to burst; 6. anthropologist: human; 7. creed: to believe, to put trust in; 8. Genesis: birth, kind; 9. minimize: little, less

Evaluating Your Learning (p. 267)

Answers may vary.

Chapter 9

Word Selection (p. 270)

1. adults; 2. bond; 3. priority; 4. assemble; 5. commission; 6. labor; 7. benefits

Vocabulary in Context (p. 271)

1. a; 2. c; 3. b; 4. d; 5. c; 6. c

Dictionary Use (p. 272)

Answers may vary.

1.   correspond: to be similar or compared closely, to be equal to something
2.   differentiate: to distinguish, to understand the difference

3.   distribute: to allot, to give out, to divide among

4.   encounter: to meet

5.   equate: to make equal, to treat as equal

6.   hierarchy: a system of church government by clergy in graded ranks

7.   mode: method, form, a way of doing something

Pre-Reading (p. 274)

1.   1 Peter 2:9: a chosen people, a royal priesthood, a holy nation, a people belonging to God

Ephesians 2:19–22: fellow citizens with God's people, members of God's household, the whole building, a holy temple, a dwelling in which God lives

2.   Answers may vary. The meaning, purpose, and activity of the church as established by God.

3.   1. f; 2. j; 3. l; 4. h; 5. c; 6. i; 7. m; 8. b; 9. e; 10. n; 11. a; 12. d; 13. g; 14. k

Understanding the Reading (p. 276)

1.   planting, vineyard, temple, household, olive tree, city, and people

2.   a.   The church is a fact established by God (¶ 3).

Detail 1: It is a supernatural act of God recorded in both the Old and New Testaments.

Detail 2: At Pentecost God established the church (3 miracles).

b.   The church is the place where God acts for our salvation (¶ 4).

Detail 1: The Lord encounters people, changes them, and brings them to peace with himself.

Detail 2: As we observe the outward functioning of the Word and the sacraments, we contemplate the activity of God with faith.

c.   God's acts in the church are in Christ Jesus (¶ 5–6).

Detail 1: The King-Messiah and the people of God belong together.

Detail 2: By the one Holy Spirit we are all given a special function in his body.

Pre-Reading (p. 277)

1.   1. n; 2. d; 3. a; 4. i; 5. h; 6. b; 7. l; 8. g; 9. c; 10. m; 11. e; 12. j; 13. k; 14. f

Understanding the Reading (p. 280)

2.   Answers may vary.

4.   Answers may vary.

b.   Sample outline:

I.   **The Life of the Church**

A.   Worship: the primary function of the church (¶ 1)

B.   Fellowship: the life of the church between Jesus Christ and the believers (¶ 2–4)

C.   Witness: the task of the church (¶ 6)

II.   The Ministry of the Church

A.   The priesthood of believers (¶ 9–10)

B.   The ministry of the Word (¶ 11)

C.   The administration of discipline (¶ 12)

D.   The oversight of property and finance (¶ 13)

E.   The ordination of ministers (¶ 14–15)

c.   Sample list of main points:

- Three aspects of the life of the church are worship, fellowship, and witness.

- Worship is the primary function of the church.

- Fellowship refers to the sharing, love, and unity of God's people.

- The task of the church is to witness, thus doing the ministry of Jesus Christ in the world.

- The ministry of the church is carried out both by those in leadership and by all believers.

- Three essential tasks of ministry are the ministry of the Word, the administration of discipline, and the oversight of property and finance.

- Ordination is the rite that recognizes the appointment of certain people as ministers.

d.   Sample questions:

Q: What are three aspects of the life of the church?

A: worship, fellowship, witness

Q: Who should do the ministry of the church?

A: everyone, which includes the official ministers and the church members

Q: What are three tasks of ministry?

A: preaching and teaching the Word of God, the carrying out of discipline, and the handling of church property and finances

Exercises (pp. 281–282)

2.   1.   Since this is (how) Christ loves them . . . SC

2.   In his wisdom God has provided (that) there should be such ministers in the church. DO

3.   (That) the Christian life must be lived under the control of the same Spirit is also clear. S

4.   The reality for human beings is (that) all have sinned and are guilty before God. SC

5.   (What) happens is often described in the New Testament with words such as . . . S

6.   This does not necessarily mean (that) all local churches will do everything. DO

7. It illustrates(how)we can become part of the family of God. DO
8. This is(what)is meant by justification. SC
9. Christians are to experience mutual encouragement in doing(what)is right. DO
10. The biblical understanding is(that)in salvation something has happened ... SC
11. "(Whoever)believes in the Son has eternal life" (Jn 3:36). S
12. God has sovereignly determined or foreordained(whatever)comes to pass. DO
13. "(Whoever)does the will of my Father in heaven is my brother and sister ..." (Mt 12:50). S
14. Christ taught(who)he was and(why)he came. DO, DO
15. "This is(how)we know(what)love is: Jesus Christ laid down his life for us ..." (1 Jn 3:16). SC, DO

Exercises (pp. 282–283)

1. 1. God is acting to bring all of creation to the(place)where it finds its true head in Christ.
   2. It is a(task)which involves much sacrifice and suffering.
   3. Loving fellowship provides the context for(discipline)that is more preventive than corrective.
   4. Luke reports the(process)by which they came to their conclusions.
   5. He has planned for and anticipates the(consummation)when his work is completed.
   6. It consists of the community of(believers)who acknowledge and confess the orthodox faith.
      Alternate answer:(community of believers)
   7. The fullest revelation of salvation is in the(New Testament)where the work of Christ is applied to human lives and their most critical need.
   8. Both the Old and New Testaments use Abraham as the great example of(one)whose faith and trust in God was credited to him as righteousness.
   9. It is(he)who broke down the(barrier)that had kept Jews and Gentiles apart.
   10. There is tension because they are living between the great arrival of the(kingdom of God)which came through the ministry of Christ and the future(consummation)when God's purposes will be fulfilled. They live as pilgrims, (aliens)who are living in this world but not as part of its system.

2. 1. assumed that Christianity and Judaism were inseparable   NC
   2. assumed . . . that one must become a Jew   NC
   3. demonstrating that he made no distinction between Jews and Gentiles NC

4. citing evidence . . . that God had always intended to accept Gentiles AC

5. affirmed that salvation is a gift of God's grace   NC

6. requirements that avoided placing unnecessary burdens upon Gentile believers   AC

7. truth that God alone is to be worshiped   AC

8. the fact that believers are to conform their life and conduct   AC

9. matters that can be addressed within the context of Christian freedom AC

Exercise (p. 284)

1. God's call works in an effective way so as to bring about the salvation of the human (being) to whom his call is directed. R
   Alternate answer: (human being)

2. In the New Testament it is (Jesus Christ) who is the sacrifice for our sins. R

3. "He is the (stone) you builders rejected, which has become the capstone'" (Acts 4:11). NR

4. "Salvation belongs to our (God) who sits on the throne, and to the Lamb" (Rev 7:10). NR

5. The NT (concept) that Jesus Christ is the propitiation for our sins is a reflection of the OT sacrificial system. R
   Alternate answer: (NT concept)

6. The (Holy Spirit) who brought us from death in trespasses and sin into life and union with Jesus Christ, is also the agent of sanctification. NR

7. "God made (him) who had no sin to be sin for us . . ." (2 Cor 5:21). R

8. Paul speaks of the man (Christ Jesus) who gave himself as a ransom for all people. NR

9. It will be the (time) when believers are fully conformed to the image and likeness of Jesus Christ. R

10. Paul began talking with the (citizens) of Athens, whose favorite pastime was to discuss new ideas. NR
    Alternate answer: (citizens of Athens)

11. The Holy Spirit regenerates or re-creates fallen (human nature) which is spiritually dead. NR

12. Salvation is often described in the New Testament with words such as *righteousness* and *justification*, (terms) which reflect the administration of law and justice. R

13. Jesus Christ's righteousness is credited to (those) who believe on him. R.

14. Efficacious grace is (grace) that achieves the (purpose) for which it is given. R, R

Exercise (p. 285)

1. (miracles and wonders) God had done among the Gentiles; that/which

2. (a people) saved by the Lord; who; are

3. (James) the brother of Jesus; who; was
4. (principles) rooted in the nature of God; that/which; are
5. (Creator) possessing full claim over everything he made; who; possesses
6. (favor of God) encompassing his provision of salvation; that/which; encompasses
7. (name) derived from the Hebrew Joshua; that/which; was/is
8. (Peter) filled with the Holy Spirit; who; was
9. (calling) you have received; that/which

Pre-Reading (pp. 285–286)

1. Answers may vary.
2. Answers may vary.
3. Sacramentalist View, Covenantal View, Ordinance View
4. Episcopal or Monarchial, Presbyterian, Congregational, Other

Understanding the Reading (pp. 293–295)

1. Answers may vary for rewritten items.
    1. TRUE
    2. TRUE
    3. FALSE: Most Protestant churches recognize only two sacraments, baptism and the Lord's Supper.
    4. TRUE
    5. TRUE
    6. FALSE: The Presbyterian form of church government elects elders who lead through a representative administrative structure.
    7. TRUE
    8. TRUE
    9. TRUE
    10. FALSE: The Holy Spirit dwells in the church through individual believers and the collective body of believers.
    11. TRUE
    12. TRUE
    13. FALSE: The Lord's Supper was established by Christ to practice the commemoration of his death until he comes again.
    14. TRUE
    15. FALSE: Transubstantiation is the traditional Roman Catholic view of the Lord's Supper.
    16. FALSE: Zwingli believed that since Christ ascended in bodily form, the words, "this is my body . . . my blood" have only a figurative meaning.
    17. TRUE

2. Sacramental View

> Significance: the means by which one is transformed from spiritual death to life
>
> Mode of Baptism: not tied to one form

Covenantal View

> Significance: a sign and seal of God's working out his covenant with his people
>
> Mode of Baptism: not limited to one mode

Ordinance View

> Significance: an outward symbol of an inward change
>
> Mode of Baptism: immersion

3. Answers may vary. The visible church is what we can see. It can include a mix of those regenerate and unregenerate, as well as some hypocrisy and deceit. The invisible church is the true church, and is made up of all believers whose names are written in the Lamb's Book of Life.

Reviewing Theological Vocabulary (pp. 295–296)

1. a; 2. b; 3. c; 4. d; 5. a; 6. b; 7. b; 8. d; 9. b; 10. a

Reviewing Adjective Clauses (p. 297)

1. Restoration is impossible without God's (grace,) which is unmerited favor of God towards his creation.

2. (Abraham,) who resided in Ur of the Chaldees, was a worshiper of other gods when God appeared to him.

3. ". . . It is by the name of (Jesus Christ) of Nazareth, whom you crucified . . . that this man stands before you healed" (Acts 4:10).
   Alternate answer: (Jesus Christ of Nazareth)

4. The (Christian life,) which is the new life of the believer, is made available by the triune God.

5. The (passage) that she read to the class was John 17:14–17.

6. The invisible church consists of all (those) whose names are written in the Lamb's Book of Life.

7. There are many (situations) for which there is no direct divine guidance in Scripture.

8. (Choices and decisions) that are made in daily life should be consistent with biblical principles.

9. A less common word is ("imputation,") which is a bookkeping term.

10. (Those) who are led by the Spirit are spoken of as "sons of God" or "children of God."

11. The (life) we live in Christ has eternal sacrifice.

12. (Those) responsible for cooking the meal were tired after the church supper.

Evaluating Your Learning (pp. 297–298)

Answers may vary.

Chapter 10

Word Forms (pp. 300–301)

1. emerges, verb; 2. corporate, adjective; 3. guarantee, noun; 4. intermediate, adjective; 5. motive, noun; 6. implementing, verb

Vocabulary in Context (pp. 301–302)

1. b; 2. d; 3. a; 4. a; 5. c; 6. b; 7. c

Word Definitions (pp. 302–303)

Answers may vary.

1. controversy: public dispute, argument
2. ensures: makes certain
3. ongoing: continuing, actually in process
4. nevertheless: in spite of that, all the same
5. founded: to lay the base of; guaranteed: assured, promises that a thing will be done
6. contradictions: inconsistencies, conditions that are contrary to each other
7. challenge: a demanding task that calls for special effort and dedication

Pre-Reading: Entire Article (p. 304)

1.
   - I. The OT perspective
   - II. The NT perspective
   - III. Christian life in hope
   - IV. Signs of the times
   - V. The coming of Christ
   - VI. The resurrection
   - VII. The state of the dead
   - VIII. The judgment
   - IX. Hell
   - X. The millennium
   - XI. The new creation

2. Answers may vary. Example: What is the OT perspective of eschatology?

Pre-Reading: Introduction and Sections I–III (pp. 304–305)

1. Eschatology (the doctrine of the last things) is the study of how God's purposes, revealed by his redemptive acts in history, are fulfilled at the consummation.
2. 1. d; 2. h; 3. f; 4. k; 5. b; 6. i; 7. n; 8. l; 9. c; 10. m; 11. p; 12. e; 13. g; 14. j; 15. a; 16. o; 17. q

Understanding the Reading (p. 309)

1. Answers may vary.

2. Answers may vary. Examples: eschatology, the Day of the Lord, one like a son of man, inaugurated eschatology, already and not yet, kingdom of God

3. Inaugurated eschatology refers to a 'realized' and 'future' aspect of New Testament eschatology which is found in Jesus' proclamation of the kingdom of God. In Jesus' own person and mission, the kingdom of God is present, demanding response, so that a person's participation in the future kingdom is determined by his/her response to Jesus in the present.

4. "Already" refers to the work of Christ that has been done. The Lamb of God was slain and his death is a decisive victory. "Not yet" refers to the final outworking of this victory, which will come in the future. We share in Jesus' risen life now (already), but a future resurrection to life awaits the believer (not yet).

Pre-Reading: Sections IV–VIII (pp. 309–310)

1. Answers may vary. Examples: Signs of the times and The coming of Christ.

2. The asterisk (*) marks the words in the article that have their own entries in the *New Bible Dictionary*. They are marked because the editor thought that the other entries would be helpful for understanding the "Eschatology" entry.

3. 1. f; 2. r; 3. a; 4. q; 5. p; 6. g; 7. h; 8. j; 9. n; 10. o; 11. m; 12. c; 13. k; 14. b; 15. i; 16. e; 17. l; 18. d

Understanding the Reading (pp. 314–315)

1. Answers may vary.

2. Answers may vary. Examples: imminence, delay of the *parousia*, Antichrist, *parousia*, *apokalypsis*, *epiphaneia*, resurrection, immortality, the spirits in prison, intermediate state, judgment, justification

3. "The day of the Lord" refers to the coming event of God's decisive action in judgment and salvation. A similar phrase is "on that day."

4. *parousia*: coming; *apokalypsis*: revelation, unveiling, disclosure; *epiphaneia*: appearing

Pre-Reading: Sections IX–XI and Bibliography (p. 315)

2. 1. l; 2. h; 3. e; 4. n; 5. j; 6. c; 7. a; 8. m; 9. k; 10. f; 11. g; 12. b; 13. d; 14. i

Understanding the Reading (p. 318)

1. Answers may vary. Examples: hell, *Gehenna*, millennium, premillennialism, dispensationalism, new creation, new Jerusalem

2. Answers may vary.

Pre-Reading (p. 319)

Answers may vary.

3. The three views are premillennialism, postmillennialism, and amillennialism.

4.   Sample outline:
 I. **Introduction**
  A. Difficulty of interpreting Revelation
  B. Need to figure out author's intent
 II. **The Preterist View**
  A. Intended for the first century church
  B. Prophecies fulfilled in the first century
  C. Accepted by a wide spectrum of people
   1. Nineteenth century liberalism
   2. Christian Reconstructionism
   3. Critical scholarship
 III. **The Historicist (Historical) View**
  A. Prophecy of the history and destiny of the church
  B. Meaningful to later generations, not early Christians
 IV. **The Idealist View**
  A. Spiritual/symbolic interpretation
  B. Not concerned with actual circumstances
 V. **The Futurist View**
  A. Concerned with the end times
  B. Takes seriously the predictive element of Revelation

Understanding the Reading (p. 327)

1. intermediate state; 2. general resurrection; 3. idealist view; 4. dispensationalism;
5. historicist view; 6. amillennialism; 7. eternal life; 8. annihilationism; 9. preterist
view; 10. postmillennialism; 11. death

Reviewing Theological Vocabulary (pp. 328–329)

1. d; 2. c; 3. d; 4. a; 5. b; 6. a; 7. c; 8. b; 9. d; 10. a; 11. d; 12. c

Evaluating Your Learning (p. 329)

Answers may vary.

Appendixes, Notes, and References

Appendix 1
English Proficiency Levels

Comparison of Four Proficiency Measures

The ACTFL Proficiency Guidelines describe four levels of language ability and ten sub-levels for each of the four skills (listening, speaking, reading, writing) (http://www.actfl.org). They are similar to the Foreign Service Institute (FSI) or Interagency Language Roundtable (ILR) proficiency levels for each of the four skills (http://www.utm.edu/~globeg/ilrhome.shtml). Two similar sets of guidelines are the Centre for Canadian Language Benchmarks scale which gives twelve levels for each skill (http://www.language.ca) and the Common European Framework, now widely used across Europe (http://www.coe.int/t/dg4/linguistic/Source/Framework_EN.pdf).

These four sets of proficiency guidelines are highly useful for planning the areas of focus and specific activities to include in a learning program as well as evaluating overall proficiency, including the learners' ability to handle real-life tasks in a second language. The Common European Framework and Canadian Language Benchmarks provide the most detailed information, generally making them more useful for teachers than the other two scales.

	FSI / ILR	ACTFL	Common European Framework	Canadian Language Benchmarks	
PROFICIENCY LEVEL	5 (functionally native proficiency)			Stage 3: Advanced	
	4+ (advanced professional proficiency, plus)	Superior	C-2		12
	4 (advanced professional proficiency)				11
	3+ (general professional proficiency, plus)		C-1		10
	3 (general professional proficiency)				9
	2+ (limited working proficiency, plus)	Advanced High	B-2+	Stage 2: Intermediate	8
	2 (limited working proficiency)	Advanced Mid	B-2		7
		Advanced Low	B-1+		6
	1+ (elementary proficiency, plus)	Intermediate High	B-1		5–6
	1 (elementary proficiency)	Intermediate Mid	A-2+	Stage 1: Basic	4
		Intermediate Low	A-2		3
	0+ (memorized proficiency)	Novice High	A-1+		2
	0 (no proficiency)	Novice Mid	A-1		2
		Novice Low			1

Needs Analysis Checklist

A checklist such as this one is useful for determining the areas where your students believe that they should receive the most help. Although some students are not highly aware of their strengths and weaknesses, others will be able to give you valuable information. Furthermore, nearly all students appreciate being asked about their needs.

Rather than using all of the items from this checklist, we suggest that you first think carefully about your students and their needs. Then by modifying, deleting, and adding items, you can make it more appropriate for your learners.

What do you need to learn?	Very Important	Important	Not Very Important
1. understanding common English words			
2. understanding academic words			
3. understanding biblical terms that I know in my native language but I don't know in English			
4. understanding long sentences			
5. understanding complex sentences			
6. understanding charts and diagrams			
7. reading more quickly			
8. reading without having to use a dictionary so often			
9. using a bilingual dictionary			
10. using an English-only dictionary			
11. taking notes when I read			
12. making an outline			

13. remembering what I read			
14.			
15.			

From this list, which two areas will help you the most when you are reading theological materials?

1. _____

2. _____

Appendix 3

Basic English Vocabulary

The *General Service List of English Words (GSL)* (West 1953) consists of about 2,000 word families that are used frequently in spoken and written English. ESL/EFL teachers should make sure that their students master these words before focusing on academic vocabulary (e.g., the Coxhead Academic Word List), technical or discipline-specific vocabulary (e.g., theological vocabulary), and low-frequency words. You can find this widely used word list on a number of Web sites such as http://jbauman.com/aboutgsl.html and http://www.nottingham.ac.uk/~alzsh3/acvocab/wordlists.htm.

The First 1000 Words of the General Service List

a	alone	attack	between	business	clear
able	along	attempt	beyond	but	clock
about	already	average	big	buy	close
above	also	away	bill	by	club
accept	although	back	bird	call	coast
accord	always	bad	bit	can	cold
account	among	ball	black	capital	college
across	amount	bank	blood	car	colour
act	ancient	bar	blow	care	come
actual	and	base	blue	carry	command
add	animal	battle	board	case	common
address	another	be	boat	catch	company
admit	answer	bear	body	cause	compare
adopt	any	beauty	book	centre	complete
advance	appear	because	born	certain	concern
advantage	apply	become	both	chance	condition
affair	appoint	bed	box	change	connect
afford	arise	before	boy	character	consider
after	arm	begin	branch	charge	contain
again	army	behind	bread	chief	content
against	around	being	breadth	child	continue
age	arrive	believe	break	choose	control
ago	art	belong	bridge	church	corner
agree	article	below	bright	circle	cost
air	as	beneath	bring	city	could
all	ask	beside	brother	claim	council
allow	association	best	build	class	count
almost	at	better	burn	clean	country

course	doubt	experience	form	hear	keep
court	down	experiment	former	heat	kill
cover	draw	explain	forth	heaven	kind
creature	dream	express	fortune	heavy	know
cross	dress	extend	forward	help	lack
crowd	drive	eye	free	her	lady
cry	drop	face	friend	here	land
current	dry	fact	from	hide	language
custom	due	factory	front	high	large
cut	during	fail	full	hill	last
dance	each	fair	further	his	late
danger	ear	faith	future	history	law
dare	early	fall	gain	hold	lay
dark	earth	familiar	game	home	lead
date	east	family	garden	honour	learn
daughter	easy	famous	gate	hope	least
day	eat	farm	gather	horse	leave
dead	edge	fashion	general	hot	left
deal	effect	fast	gentle	hour	length
decide	effort	father	get	house	less
declare	either	favourite	give	how	let
deep	else	favour	glad	hullo	letter
degree	employ	fear	glass	human	level
deliver	end	feed	go	hurrah	library
demand	enemy	feel	God	husband	lie
describe	English	fellow	gold	I	life
desert	enjoy	few	good	idea	lift
desire	enough	field	great	if	light
destroy	enter	figure	green	impossible	like
detail	entire	fill	ground	in	likely
determine	equal	find	group	inch	limit
develop	escape	fine	grow	include	line
die	even	finger	guard	increase	listen
difference	evening	finish	habit	indeed	little
difficult	event	fire	half	independent	live
direct	ever	first	hall	influence	local
discover	every	fish	hand	instead	long
disease	everywhere	fit	handle	intend	look
distance	evil	fix	hang	interest	lose
distinguish	example	floor	happen	into	lost
district	excellent	flower	happy	introduce	lot
divide	except	follow	hard	iron	love
do	exchange	food	hardly	it	low
doctor	exercise	for	have	its	machine
dog	exist	force	he	join	main
door	expect	foreign	head	judge	make
double	expense	forget	health	just	man

manner	nation	ought	press	relation	seize
manners	native	ounce	pretty	religion	sell
many	nature	our	prevent	remain	send
march	near	out of	price	remark	sense
mark	necessary	out	print	remember	separate
market	neck	over	private	repeat	serious
marry	need	owe	problem	reply	serve
mass	neighbour	own	produce	report	set
material	neither	page	product	represent	settle
matter	never	pain	production	respect	several
may	new	paint	program	rest	shadow
me	next	paper	programme	result	shake
mean	night	part	progress	return	shall
measure	no	party	promise	rich	shape
meet	none	pass	proof	ride	share
member	nor	past	proper	right	shave
memory	north	pay	propose	ring	she
mention	not	peace	protect	rise	shine
mere	note	people	prove	river	shoe
metal	nothing	perfect	provide	road	shoot
middle	notice	perhaps	public	roll	shore
might	now	permanent	pull	room	short
mile	nowhere	permit	purpose	rough	should
mind	number	person	put	round	shoulder
mine	object	picture	quality	rule	show
minister	observe	piece	quarter	ruler	side
minute	occasion	place	quiet	run	sight
miss	of	plan	quite	rush	sign
modern	off	plant	race	safe	silence
moment	offer	play	raise	sail	silver
money	office	please	rank	same	simple
month	often	point	rate	save	since
more	oil	political	rather	saw	single
moreover	old	poor	reach	say	sir
morning	once	popular	read	scale	sister
most	one	population	ready	scarce	sit
mother	only	position	real	scene	situation
motor	open	possess	reason	school	size
mountain	operation	possible	receive	science	skill
mouth	opinion	post	recent	sea	sky
move	opportunity	pound	recognize	season	sleep
much	or	poverty	record	seat	slight
music	order	power	red	second	slow
must	ordinary	practical	reduce	secret	small
my	organize	prepare	refuse	secretary	smile
name	other	present	regard	see	so
narrow	otherwise	preserve	regular	seem	society

soft	stop	take	total	vote	win
soil	store	talk	touch	wait	wind
some	storm	taste	toward/s	walk	window
son	story	teach	town	wall	wing
soon	straight	tear	trade	want	winter
sort	strange	tell	train	war	wise
sound	stream	term	travel	warn	wish
south	street	terrible	tree	waste	with
space	strength	test	trouble	watch	within
speak	stretch	than	trust	water	without
special	strike	that	truth	wave	woman
speed	strong	the	try	way	wonder
spend	struggle	their	turn	we	wood
spirit	study	them	type	weak	word
spite	subject	then	under	wear	work
spot	substance	there	understand	week	world
spread	succeed	therefore	union	welcome	worse
spring	such	these	unite	well	worth
square	sudden	they	university	west	would
stage	suffer	thing	unless	what	write
stand	suggest	think	until	when	wrong
standard	summer	this	up	where	year
start	sun	though	upon	whether	yellow
state	supply	thought	use	which	yes
station	support	through	usual	while	yesterday
stay	suppose	throw	valley	white	yet
steal	sure	thus	value	who	you
steel	surface	time	various	whose	young
step	surprise	to	very	why	
stick	surround	today	view	wide	
still	sweet	together	village	wife	
stock	system	too	visit	wild	
stone	table	top	voice	will	

The Second 1000 Words of the General Service List

abroad	attend	block	cart	compete	curve
absence	attract	boast	castle	complain	cushion
absolutely	audience	boil	cat	complicated	damage
accident	aunt	bold	cattle	compose	damp
accuse	autumn	bone	caution	confess	deaf
accustom	avenue	border	cave	confidence	dear
ache	avoid	borrow	cent	confuse	debt
admire	awake	bottle	century	congratulate	decay
adventure	awkward	bottom	ceremony	conquer	deceive
advertise	axe	bound	chain	conscience	decrease
advice	baby	boundary	chair	conscious	deed
afraid	bag	bow	chalk	convenience	deer
afternoon	baggage	bowl	charm	conversation	defeat
agent	bake	brain	cheap	cook	defend
agriculture	balance	brass	cheat	cool	delay
ahead	band	brave	check	copper	delicate
aim	barber	breakfast	cheer	copy	delight
aeroplane	bare	breath	cheese	cork	department
alike	bargain	bribe	cheque	corn	depend
alive	barrel	brick	chest	correct	descend
aloud	basin	broad	chicken	cottage	deserve
altogether	basket	brown	chimney	cotton	desk
ambition	bath	brush	Christmas	cough	despair
amongst	bay	bucket	civilize	courage	devil
amuse	beak	bunch	clay	cousin	diamond
anger	beam	bundle	clerk	cow	dictionary
angle	bean	burst	clever	coward	dig
annoy	beard	bury	cliff	crack	dinner
anxiety	beast	bus	climb	crash	dip
apart	beat	bush	cloth	cream	dirt
apologize	beg	busy	cloud	creep	disappoint
applaud	behave	butter	coal	crime	discipline
apple	bell	button	coarse	critic	discuss
approve	belt	cage	coat	crop	disgust
arch	bend	cake	coffee	crown	dish
argue	berry	calculate	coin	cruel	dismiss
arrange	bicycle	calm	collar	crush	disturb
arrest	bind	camera	collect	cultivate	ditch
arrow	birth	camp	colony	cup	dive
artificial	bite	canal	comb	cupboard	dollar
ash	bitter	cap	combine	cure	donkey
ashamed	blade	cape	comfort	curious	dot
aside	blame	captain	commerce	curl	dozen
asleep	bless	card	committee	curse	drag
astonish	blind	carriage	companion	curtain	drawer

drink	fate	generous	horizon	juice	mad
drown	fault	girl	hospital	jump	mail
drum	feast	glory	host	key	male
duck	feather	goat	hotel	kick	manage
dull	female	govern	humble	king	manufacture
dust	fence	grace	hunger	kiss	map
duty	fever	gradual	hunt	kitchen	master
eager	fierce	grain	hurry	knee	mat
earn	fight	grammar	hurt	kneel	match
earnest	film	grand	hut	knife	meal
ease	firm	grass	ice	knock	meanwhile
educate	flag	grateful	ideal	knot	meat
efficient	flame	grave	idle	ladder	mechanic
egg	flash	grease	ill	lake	medicine
elastic	flat	greed	imagine	lamp	melt
elder	flavour	greet	imitate	latter	mend
elect	flesh	grey	immediate	laugh	merchant
electricity	float	grind	immense	lazy	mercy
elephant	flood	guess	important	leaf	merry
empire	flour	guest	improve	lean	message
empty	flow	guide	indoors	leather	mild
enclose	fly	guilty	industry	leg	milk
encourage	fold	gun	inform	lend	mill
engine	fond	hair	ink	lessen	miserable
entertain	fool	hammer	in-law	lesson	mistake
envelope	foot	handkerchief	inn	liberty	mix
envy	forbid	harbour	inquire	lid	model
especial	forest	harm	insect	limb	moderate
essence	forgive	harvest	inside	lip	modest
exact	fork	haste	instant	liquid	monkey
examination	formal	hat	instrument	list	moon
excess	frame	hate	insult	literature	moral
excite	freeze	hay	insure	load	motion
excuse	frequent	heal	interfere	loaf	mouse
explode	fresh	heap	international	loan	mud
explore	fright	heart	interrupt	lock	multiply
extra	fruit	height	invent	lodging	murder
extraordinary	fry	hesitate	invite	log	mystery
extreme	fun	hinder	inward/s	lonely	nail
fade	funeral	hire	island	loose	neat
faint	fur	hit	jaw	lord	needle
false	furnish	hole	jealous	loud	neglect
fan	gallon	holiday	jewel	loyal	nephew
fancy	gap	hollow	joint	luck	nest
far	garage	holy	joke	lump	net
farther	gas	honest	journey	lunch	nice
fat	gay	hook	joy	lung	niece

noble	pet	pronounce	resign	scissors	snow
noise	photograph	property	resist	scold	soap
nonsense	pick	proud	responsible	scorn	socks
noon	pig	pump	restaurant	scrape	soldier
nose	pigeon	punctual	retire	scratch	solemn
noun	pile	punish	revenge	screen	solid
nuisance	pin	pupil	review	screw	solve
nurse	pinch	pure	reward	search	sore
nut	pink	purple	ribbon	seed	sorry
oar	pint	push	rice	seldom	soul
obey	pipe	puzzle	rid	sentence	soup
ocean	pity	qualify	ripe	severe	sour
offend	plain	quantity	risk	sew	sow
omit	plaster	quarrel	rival	shade	spade
onto	plate	quart	roar	shallow	spare
opposite	plenty	queen	roast	shame	spell
orange	plough	question	rob	sharp	spill
organ	plural	quick	rock	sheep	spin
origin	pocket	rabbit	rod	sheet	spit
ornament	poet	radio	roof	shelf	splendid
overcome	poison	rail	root	shell	split
pack	police	rain	rope	shelter	spoil
pad	polish	rake	rot	shield	spoon
pair	polite	rapid	row	shilling	sport
pale	pool	rare	royal	ship	staff
pan	postpone	rat	rub	shirt	stain
parcel	pot	raw	rubber	shock	stairs
pardon	pour	ray	rubbish	shop	stamp
parent	powder	razor	rude	shout	star
park	practice	recommend	rug	shower	steady
particular	praise	refer	ruin	shut	steam
passage	pray	reflect	rust	sick	steep
paste	preach	refresh	sacred	signal	steer
path	precious	regret	sacrifice	silk	stem
patient	prefer	rejoice	sad	sincere	stiff
patriotic	prejudice	relieve	saddle	sing	sting
pattern	president	remedy	sake	sink	stir
pause	pretend	remind	salary	skin	stockings
paw	pride	rent	sale	skirt	stomach
pearl	priest	repair	salt	slave	stove
peculiar	prison	replace	sample	slide	strap
pen	prize	reproduce	sand	slip	straw
pencil	probable	republic	satisfy	slope	strict
penny	procession	reputation	sauce	smell	string
per	profession	request	saucer	smoke	strip
perform	profit	rescue	scatter	smooth	stripe
persuade	prompt	reserve	scent	snake	stuff

stupid	telephone	tie	treasure	veil	wheel
suck	temper	tight	treat	verb	whip
sugar	temperature	till	tremble	verse	whisper
suit	temple	tin	trial	vessel	whistle
supper	tempt	tip	tribe	victory	whole
suspect	tend	tire	trick	violent	wicked
swallow	tender	title	trip	virtue	widow
swear	tent	tobacco	true	vowel	wine
sweat	thank/s	toe	trunk	voyage	wipe
sweep	theatre	tomorrow	tube	wage/s	wire
swell	thick	ton	tune	waist	witness
swim	thief	tongue	twist	wake	wool
swing	thin	tonight	ugly	wander	worm
sword	thirst	tool	umbrella	warm	worry
sympathy	thorn	tooth	uncle	wash	worship
tail	thorough	tough	unit	wax	wound
tailor	thread	tour	unity	wealth	wrap
tall	threaten	towel	universe	weapon	wreck
tame	throat	tower	upper	weather	wrist
tap	thumb	toy	upright	weave	yard
tax	thunder	track	upset	weed	yield
taxi	ticket	translate	upwards	weigh	zero
tea	tide	trap	urge	wet	
telegraph	tidy	tray	vain	wheat	

ESL/EFL Student Resources

ESL/EFL students often want to go beyond the instruction provided by *ETE* in order to expand their knowledge of the language. To help them select appropriate textbooks and supplementary materials, Appendix 4 in the student text (*ETE*, pp. 357–361) lists a number of recommended resources.

This *TG* appendix differs in two ways from the one in the student text: Because this section is written for ESL/EFL teachers, we begin with a discussion of the three essential steps in the process of textbook evaluation and selection. We include this information because publishers offer dozens of textbook choices for almost every imaginable aspect of English teaching, and your challenge will be knowing which books will best meet the learning needs your students. Then, we list specific resources that are useful for teaching a variety of ESL/EFL skills and components. This is a broader list than the one found in the student text. Here we include additional textbooks and Web sites for learning reading, vocabulary, and grammar, and we also include resources for listening, speaking, pronunciation, composition, and IELTS and TOEFL test preparation. In addition to resources for learners of academic English, we include some items for learners who are at lower proficiency levels in English.

Textbook Evaluation and Selection[1]

To make a well-informed decision about textbook selection, you should know some information about your students' needs, your instructional objectives, and your personal teaching preferences. We list a number of questions to guide you through this assessment process. Although you may not be able to find a satisfactory answer for each question, the answers you do find—as well as the additional information you gather in the process—will be of considerable benefit in evaluating and selecting materials appropriate for your teaching situation.

Know your students' needs

An invaluable first step in the selection of materials is to gather information about your students' language learning needs and preferences. Although you may want to collect a much wider range of information, we suggest that you begin with these four categories: language background, proficiency level, learning goals, and preferred approaches to learning. Before using these questions, modify them as needed.

Language background: previous experiences with their native language and with English

- What type and level of general academic study have they done in their native language?
- Have they studied theology in their native language?
- In what settings have they studied English (e.g., classroom, tutoring, self-study)?
- Have they studied the Bible (or Bible and theology) in English?

Proficiency level in English

- What is their current proficiency level in English?
- Are all students at the same level?
- Are they stronger in some skills (e.g., reading and writing) and weaker in others (e.g., listening and speaking)?

Learning goals

- Do they use English only for reading, or reading and a limited amount of writing?
- Do they need to write academic papers in English?
- Do they need English for listening and speaking?
- If they require oral communication skills, with whom will they speak English? For example, will they use the language only in the classroom, will they use it outside of class for general communication?
- What tasks do they want to accomplish in English? For example. will they need it in order to understand lectures in English? Will they need to use it in classroom discussions or for making oral presentations?

Preferred approaches to learning

- Are they accustomed to a more traditional, teacher-centered classroom in which most interaction is between teacher and student (not student to student), or are they more comfortable in a learner-centered classroom in which students interact with one another in pairs and small groups?
- Do they like language learning activities in which they have an opportunity to communicate freely even though they may make mistakes, or do they prefer the study of grammar and an emphasis on accuracy of speech and writing?

The answers to these questions will provide one type of information essential for choosing materials that are suitable for your particular students. For example, if you are a new teacher in a country where much of your students' previous instruction involved rote memorization of facts, you may not want to begin your teaching with a textbook that is strongly communicative or one that has little emphasis on grammar and accuracy. Frequently, a more communicative textbook will be better received after you have gained your students' trust, and after you have employed activities such as pair work and role play gradually over time.

Know your instructional objectives

Taking the time to clearly define your objectives—or to understand the list of objectives provided by the institution in which you teach—will greatly limit the scope of your search for the right textbook. To do this, you should ask questions such as this:

- Given my students' language background, proficiency level, learning goals, and preferred approaches to learning, what can I realistically expect them to be able to do as a result of my English instruction?

Then move from their needs to teaching objectives:

- Make a list of general objectives (e.g., understand the readings in the textbook) and for each, try to list two or three specific objectives (e.g., learn the important theological vocabulary; explain the theological concepts in your native language).

With a list of objectives in hand, you can narrow your textbook selection considerably. You do this by matching your objectives with the proficiency level, content focus, and activity types of a number of potential choices. You may find, for example, that your preferred text should have a heavy emphasis on grammar. Or, you may discover that it should focus entirely on oral communication skills, including pronunciation, but have little or no emphasis on grammar.

Know your personal teaching preferences

The third step in the selection process is the assessment of your own teaching style and teaching preferences. To help you to think about the teaching-learning environment that is most ideal for you, as well as your expectations of a textbook, you can begin with questions such as these:

Classroom environment: roles of teacher and students

- What teacher role(s) suit your personality and teaching style? Do you prefer the role of director (one who carefully guides students in their learning exercises and activities, usually having them interact more with you than with each other), the role of facilitator (one who organizes and monitors pair work and small group work), or some combination of these roles?

The "fit" between teaching style and textbook choice

- How dependent are you on the textbook content for planning your lessons? For example, do you prefer to stick to the textbook, using it as your basic syllabus? Or, do you like to vary your approach based on the content of the lesson?
- Are you good at adapting materials and/or creating supplemental activities?

As you examine a range of textbooks, you should look for those that accentuate your strengths while also encouraging you to develop skills in new areas. For example, if you have not taught ESL/EFL before, you may prefer to begin with a text that is more teacher-centered, allowing you to be more in control of instructional activities. Then, as you get to know your students and feel more comfortable in the classroom, you may want to adapt some of the book's activities for small group work, thus creating a more learner-centered environment.

Summary
By carefully evaluating a number of textbooks in light of what you know about your students' needs, your instructional objectives, and yourself as a teacher, you will be better equipped to choose the best materials for your teaching-learning situation. For each of these three areas, we have given you a set of questions to guide your selection process. However, each set can be summarized by a single key question to ask about the textbook(s) you are considering.

- How appropriate is the book for my students' language learning needs?
- To what extent does the book focus on my instructional objectives?
- What skills do I need in order to use the book most effectively?

Teaching Materials
Although some books are for learners at the lower levels, this list focuses primarily on resources for high intermediate to advanced learners who need additional work on academic reading, vocabulary, and grammar skills as well as aspects of language other than those addressed in *ETE*. For an additional list of ESL/EFL resources for learners at all levels and/or with somewhat different needs, see the Institute for Cross-Cultural Training Web site, http://www.wheaton.edu/bgc/ICCT/ResandLinks/Annot_Biblio.html.

All Skills: Academic English
Each of the major publishers offers a range of resources for teaching the four skills (listening, speaking, reading, writing). Multi-level series such as the widely-used *Interchange* (Cambridge University Press) are for those learning General Purpose English. They usually begin with an introductory level for beginners and have an additional three to five levels. While series of this type can help learners to get a broad foundation in the language, they do not provide the type of preparation that is needed for serious academic study in English. When selecting textbooks for learners who plan to use English for part or all of their academic instruction, we encourage you to consider *English for Academic Success* or similar resources from other ESL/EFL publishers.

> *English for Academic Success* series. Boston: Houghton Mifflin (now Heinle ELT), 2006.
> Chan, Marsha. *College Oral Communication 1.*
> Roemer, Ann E. *College Oral Communication 2.*
> Delk, Cheryl L. *College Oral Communication 3.*
> Jones, Steve. *College Oral Communication 4.*

Benz, Cheryl, with Myra M. Medina. *College Reading 1.*
Robinson Fellag, Linda. *College Reading 2.*
Avery, John D., and Robinson Fellag, Linda. *College Reading 3.*
Benz, Cheryl, and Cynthia M. Schuemann. *College Reading 4.*

Walsh, Karen E. *College Writing 1.*
Cotter, Eileen. *College Writing 2.*
Nuttall, Gabriella. *College Writing 3.*
Tunceren, Li-Lee, and Sharon Cavusgil, *College Writing 4.*

Howard, Julie. *College Vocabulary 1.*
Chaudron, Gille. *College Vocabulary 2.*
Folse, Keith S., and Marcella Farina. *College Vocabulary 3.*
Bunting, John D. *College Vocabulary 4.*

Addressing the needs of four levels of learners (low intermediate, intermediate, high intermediate, high intermediate to advanced), this series is for students who are beginning with a good foundation in General Purpose English but do not yet have the academic language proficiency required for study at the college level. The series goal is to prepare students to handle the English-language demands of a college or university where all instruction is in English. To do this, each level integrates the four skills (listening, speaking, reading, writing) as it focuses on content and learning activities that are similar to those found in introductory college-level textbooks from a variety of disciplines. Throughout the series, students practice using the 570 word families in the Academic Word List. The support package includes the four *Essentials* books for teachers (see *TG* Appendix 5, pp. 134-142), audio materials for the oral communication books, student Web sites with additional practice exercises, and Instructor Web sites with a variety of assessments, teaching notes, sample syllabi, answer keys, classroom handouts, and assessments.

Although this series is designed to teach the four skills, you do not need to use all four strands. For example, you might want to use only the reading and vocabulary books. In addition, if your learners are weaker in one or more skills, you will probably need to use supplementary resources such as those listed below. To find additional published materials for your students, we suggest that you look in libraries and bookstores. Then check the Web sites for the major publishers to see their offerings. (See *ETE* Appendix 4, pp. 360-361, for a list of major ESL/EFL publishers.) You can also find a large number of learning materials on the Internet.

Grammar and Vocabulary

See *ETE* Appendix 4, pp. 357–361, for recommended grammar and vocabulary resources. In addition, you may want to consider the following resources:

Larsen-Freeman, Diane, series ed. *Grammar Dimensions: Form, Meaning, and Use*, 4th ed. Boston: Heinle ELT, 2007–2008.

This popular grammar series is rich in content and up-to-date in its contextualized practice. With four levels ranging from beginning to advanced, accompanying workbooks, and split editions for shorter courses, it can be adapted for a variety of teaching situations. For each grammar point, learners practice the form, the meaning, and the use of the structure in communication. Each student text contains a CD-ROM of supplementary activities. The complete package includes teacher's edition, audiotapes, and assessment CD-ROMs.

Raimes, Ann. *Grammar Troublespots: A Guide for Student Writers*, 3d ed. Cambridge: Cambridge University Press, 2004.

For high-intermediate to low-advanced learners, this book is a guide to the most common errors students make in academic writing. Each unit provides a description of the grammar point, clear examples, grammar charts, and practice activities.

Hollinger, Lisa, Celia Thompson, Pat Bull, and Barbara Jones. *Academic Word Power*. Boston: Houghton-Mifflin (Heinle ELT), 2004.

For intermediate to high-intermediate students, this series of four books focuses on the most common words in the Academic Word List. Through a variety of exercises and activities, students encounter each word in a variety of contexts. The student Web site includes flash cards and practice tests; the instructor Web site provides unit tests, supplemental readings, and an answer key.

Listening and Speaking

Blackwell, Angela, and Therese Naber. *Open Forum: Academic Listening and Speaking*. Oxford: Oxford University Press, 2006–2007.

This three-level series helps students develop listening and speaking skills essential for participating in academic classrooms. In addition to the textbooks, there are audio CDs, audio cassettes, test booklets and answer keys, and a Web site with additional listening selections and exercises available for downloading.

Heinle ELT Listening and Notetaking Series

Dunkel, Patricia A., and Phyllis L. Lim. *Intermediate Listening Comprehension: Understanding and Recalling Spoken English*, 3d ed. Boston: Heinle ELT, 2006.

Lim, Phyllis L., and William Smalzer. *Noteworthy: Listening and Notetaking Skills*, 3d ed. Boston: Heinle ELT, 2005.

Dunkel, Patricia A., and Frank Pialorsi. *Advanced Listening Comprehension: Developing Aural and Notetaking Skills*, 3d ed. Boston: Heinle ELT, 2005.

This series prepares students to comprehend academic lectures and take notes on the main ideas and important details. Each book comes in two versions—one for use in the United States and the other for international use. The complete package includes VHS, DVD, CD, and audiotape recordings of academic lectures and other learning activities as well as an online Web site for instructors and students.

Pronunciation

Gilbert, Judy B. *Clear Speech*, 3d ed. New York: Cambridge University Press, 2005.

For intermediate to advanced students, this American English textbook focuses on the "musical" aspects of English—rhythm, stress, and intonation. Individual and paired practice activities encourage students to improve their production and comprehension skills. Also available: teacher's resource book and audio cassettes.

Grant, Linda. *Well Said: Pronunciation for Clear Communication*, 2d ed. Boston: Heinle & Heinle, 2001.

Offering a communicative approach to pronunciation learning for advanced students, this book addresses sound/spelling patterns, syllables, word endings, linking, stress, rhythm, and intonation. The complete package includes a student text, instructor's manual, audio cassettes and CD-ROMs.

Hahn, Laura D., and Wayne B. Dickerson. *Speechcraft*. Ann Arbor, MI: University of Michigan Press, 1999.

By focusing on the stress, rhythm, and melody of English words and discourse, this series of three books helps non-native English speakers interact in academic and professional settings. In addition to the core textbook are two workbooks, *Workbook for International TA Discourse* and *Workbook for Academic Discourse*, and cassette tapes.

Composition

Reid, Joy M. *The Process of Composition*, 3d ed. White Plains, NY: Pearson Longman, 1999.

This advanced level text leads students through increasingly complex academic writing tasks, starting with the paragraph, then moving to the essay, and finishing with the research paper. It provides an overall framework and then helps learners practice and refine their writing skills.

IELTS and TOEFL Preparation

Cambridge University Press offers more than a dozen sets of books and audio materials to help learners prepare for the IELTS (International English Language Testing System) Exam.

> Gear, Jolene, and Robert Gear. *Cambridge Preparation for the TOEFL Test*, 4th ed. Cambridge: Cambridge University Press, 2006.
>
> This resource prepares students for the TOEFL Test through a series of practice activities which build language and test-taking skills. It includes listening material on a CD-ROM that comes with the book. To help students gauge their progress and predict their score, seven complete TOEFL-format practice tests are included. An answer key explains why answers are correct or incorrect.

Dictionaries

Before selecting dictionaries for student use, we suggest that you look at the selection offered by two or more publishers. Each of the major publishers offers a range of dictionaries for ESL/EFL learners. These include photo and picture dictionaries for beginning and low-intermediate learners, study dictionaries that give special attention to the Coxhead Academic Word List, dictionaries for advanced learners, bilingual dictionaries, and dictionaries that focus only on idioms, phrasal verbs, or collocations.

> Lea, Diana, ed. *Oxford Collocations Dictionary for Students of English*. Oxford: Oxford University Press, 2002.
>
> Including more than 170,000 collocations, this dictionary for intermediate to advanced students shows learners how to combine words into natural-sounding phrases. (Collocations are common word combinations that go together naturally such as *speak fluently* and *meet a challenge*.)

ESL/EFL Teacher Resources

If you are new to the field of ESL/EFL teaching, you may question the importance of teacher-preparation materials. You may not sense an immediate need to read books about language learning and teaching—especially books on theory—and you may not be aware of a very large number of free resources available on the Internet. Keep in mind, however, that you can find helpful guidance in the writings of specialists in the field. You can read about everyday concerns, such as how to help learners read at a faster pace or how to foster genuine communication in the classroom. You can also address more complex issues, such as procedures for curriculum design and guidance for training new teachers. Whatever your professional concerns, you can probably find the help you need in one or more of the categories of teacher-preparation resources we list. Furthermore, as you reflect on the theoretical insights and practical ideas contained in these resources, you will develop a deeper understanding of your students and their individual learning needs and thereby become a more confident and effective ESL/EFL teacher.[1]

Foundations
Drawing upon the contributions of disciplines such as linguistics, education, and psychology, these resources provide a base of knowledge about what language is and how it is learned. They offer sound theoretical underpinnings and a principled approach for the many decisions you must make as an ESL/EFL teacher.

These two books offer an excellent overview of foundational issues and are widely used in teacher-education programs. If you plan to purchase one or more books in this category, we highly recommend these resources. However, there are many other good choices available from major publishers of ESL/EFL materials.

Brown, H. Douglas. *Principles of Language Learning and Teaching*, 5th ed. White Plains, NY: Pearson Longman, 2007.

This popular text offers an excellent analysis of major theoretical issues related to language learning and teaching. It explores topics from the theories of learning to differences between first and second language acquisition and it gives a comprehensive explanation of variables that affect language learning. Also included are an extensive updated bibliography and, at the end of each chapter, ideas for classroom application.

Lightbown, Patsy M., and Nina Spada. *How Languages are Learned*, 3d ed. Oxford: Oxford University Press, 2006.

Offering a very readable basic introduction to the main theories of first and second language acquisition, this book helps teachers understand the principles behind different teaching methodologies and discusses their practical implications for language teaching and learning.

Classroom-Oriented Principles and Methods

Resources in this category serve as a bridge between second language acquisition theory and actual classroom practice. Although some of these resources overlap with those in the first category, the focus here is on sound information to inform your instructional choices, from teaching approaches and methods, to language-learning strategies, to the effective use of a textbook.

There are dozens of very useful resources in this category, and each major publisher offers at least two or three books that address a variety of classroom issues and/or language skills. We list three books that are appropriate for teachers who are less experienced in teaching ESL/EFL (Harmer and the two books by Snow) and one that is appropriate for teachers at all levels of experience (Brown).

Brown, H. Douglas. *Teaching by Principles: An Interactive Approach to Language Pedagogy*, 3d ed. White Plains, NY: Pearson Longman, 2007.

This is a widely used teaching methodology book that presents instructional ideas in light of sound theories of second language acquisition. It includes thought-provoking questions for discussion and analysis as well as recommendations for further reading.

Harmer, Jeremy. *How to Teach English: An Introduction to the Practice of English Language Teaching*. New ed. New York: Addison Wesley Longman, 2007.

For teachers at an early stage in their careers, this book gives clear examples and explanations of current teaching practice which teachers can put to immediate use, including teaching methods and techniques, planning lessons, and using textbooks. The book also includes a DVD with video clips of good teaching practices.

Snow, Don. *From Language Learner to Language Teacher: An Introduction to Teaching English as a Foreign Language*. Alexandria, VA: TESOL, 2007.

This international edition of *More Than a Native Speaker* addresses the special needs of ESL/EFL teachers who are not native speakers of English. (See *More Than a Native Speaker*, below.)

Snow, Don. *More Than a Native Speaker: An Introduction for Volunteers Teaching Abroad.* Rev. ed. Alexandria, VA: TESOL, 2006.

This text offers highly useful, non-technical advice for new teachers, and it serves as a refresher course for experienced teachers. Easy-to-read and well-organized, it covers basic principles of language learning and teaching, course planning and individual lesson planning, the teaching of specific language skills and culture, adjustment to a new culture, and opportunities for professional development.

Teaching Resources for Specific Language Skills

Since many ESL/EFL classes focus on only one or two language components or skills (e.g., grammar, composition, or listening and speaking), many teacher resource books address only one skill or aspect of language teaching. These commonly include teaching reading, teaching writing, teaching listening/speaking or conversation, teaching grammar, teaching English for specific purposes (e.g, Business English or Medical English), cultural aspects of learning, and assessment. Many of these resources provide a variety of practical activities and games that can add to your repertoire of classroom ideas.

For each aspect of English, the major publishers offer a wide selection of books with practical information for classroom teachers. We list below only a few resources that we believe are especially useful for ESL/EFL teachers who are preparing students for academic studies in Bible and theology. Before selecting teacher resources in this category, we suggest that you check the Web sites of the major publishers to see what is currently available.

Academic English (Oral Communication, Reading, Composition, Vocabulary)

Houghton Mifflin *Essentials of Teaching Academic English* series. Boston: Houghton Mifflin, 2006. (now Heinle ELT)

Coxhead, Averil. *Essentials of Teaching Academic Vocabulary.*

Murphy, John. *Essentials of Teaching Academic Oral Communication.*

Reid, Joy M. *Essentials of Teaching Academic Writing.*

Seymour, Sharon, and Laura Walsh. *Essentials of Teaching Academic Reading.*

Each book in this series provides theoretical and practical information for teaching academic English skills. Written by scholar-teachers, these brief well-organized books offer instructors highly focused help in developing their knowledge and teaching skills. Although written to accompany the student textbooks for each of the four strands in the Houghton Mifflin *Essentials of Teaching Academic English* series, these books are also highly useful resources for teachers and teachers-in-training who are not using this series.

Grammar

Folse, Keith S. *Keys to Teaching Grammar to English Language Learners: A Practical Handbook*. Ann Arbor: University of Michigan Press, 2009.

This user-friendly introduction to English grammar teaching assumes no prior study of grammar. It offers an overview of differences between grammar for native speakers and grammar for ESL/EFL learners, a review of basic grammar terminology, information on the most common grammar points that teachers need to understand in order to help their students, answers to grammar questions ESL/EFL students ask their instructors, and techniques for teaching grammar. The accompanying workbook provides extra practice on the grammar points.

Thornbury, Scott. *How to Teach Grammar*. White Plains, NY: Pearson Longman, 2000.

A very practical resource for classroom teachers, this book addresses topics such as why grammar should be taught, how to teach it and how not to teach it, how to deal with errors, and how to integrate grammar with other language skills and components.

Listening and Speaking

Folse, Keith S. *The Art of Teaching Speaking: Research and Pedagogy for the ESL Classroom*. Ann Arbor, MI: The University of Michigan Press, 2006.

This practical book helps teachers design and use speaking tasks to promote fluency. It includes 20 case studies of successful conversation classes, detailed instructions for 20 activities, sample lesson plans, information on assessment, and appendixes that explain what conversation teachers need to know about vocabulary, pronunciation, and grammar, and how these language components affect the teaching of speaking.

Nation, I. S. P., and Jonathan Newton. *Teaching ESL/EFL Listening and Speaking*. New York and London: Routledge, 2009.

This highly useful guidebook for teachers and teachers-in-training offers a principled approach for helping learners at all levels of proficiency to develop their listening and speaking skills. It is organized around the four strands that comprise a balanced listening and speaking program: listening with a focus on comprehending meaning, speaking with a focus on conveying meaning, language-focused learning (e.g., pronunciation, spelling, vocabulary, grammar), and fluency development. (See *Teaching ESL/EFL Reading and Writing*.)

Pronunciation

Avery, Peter, and Susan Ehrlich. *Teaching American English Pronunciation.* New York: Oxford University Press, 1992.

This text helps teachers develop an understanding of the technical aspects of English phonology at the sound and phrase levels. It identifies some of the most common pronunciation problems and offers general teaching tips, and it includes a variety of techniques and types of instructional activities.

Reading and Writing

Nation, I. S. P. *Teaching ESL/EFL Reading and Writing.* New York and London: Routledge, 2009.

This is a companion text to *Teaching ESL Listening and Speaking* by Nation and Newton. It offers a principled approach for helping learners at all levels of proficiency to develop their reading and writing skills. It is organized around the four strands that comprise a balanced reading and writing program: reading with a focus on comprehending meaning, writing with a focus on conveying meaning, language-focused learning (e.g., pronunciation, spelling, vocabulary, grammar), and fluency development.

Vocabulary

Nation, I. S. P. *Learning Vocabulary in Another Language.* Cambridge: Cambridge University Press, 2001.

This frequently-cited book provides a detailed survey of research and theory on the teaching and learning of vocabulary. It contains descriptions of numerous vocabulary learning strategies, principles for vocabulary learning, and a description of what vocabulary learners at each proficiency level need to know in order to be effective users of the language. It also provides suggestions for novice and experienced practitioners who wish to design and teach a vocabulary component.

Resource Materials

Folse, Keith S. *Discussion Starters: Speaking Fluency Activities for Advanced ESL/EFL Students.* Ann Arbor, MI: The University of Michigan Press, 1996.

Each unit in this resource for intermediate to advanced learners includes exercises that provide speaking interaction about a central topic or idea. In most activities, students must work together in pairs or small groups to reach a conclusion.

Folse, Keith S., and Jeanine Ivone. *More Discussion Starters: Activities for Building Speaking Fluency.* Ann Arbor, MI: The University of Michigan Press, 2002.

Using the same format as *Discussion Starters,* this book presents additional discussion topics for intermediate to advanced students.

Ur, Penny. *Grammar Practice Activities: A Practical Guide for Teachers,* 2d ed. Cambridge: Cambridge University Press, 2009.

This very practical and widely used resource book includes an introduction to teaching grammar, guidelines for designing communicative learning activities, teaching suggestions, and a large collection of game-like learning activities for a range of levels and ages.

Ur, Penny, and Andrew Wright. *Five-Minute Activities: A Resource Book of Short Activities.* Cambridge: Cambridge University Press, 1992.

This is a popular resource with over 100 ideas for quick activities to spice up any class period. It includes activities to introduce or conclude a lesson, transition between parts of a lesson, provide extra practice for grammar or vocabulary, or simply add an element of fun. They require little preparation and can be used with students at all proficiency levels.

Wright, Andrew, David Betteridge, and Michael Buckby. *Games for Language Learning,* 3d ed. Cambridge: Cambridge University Press, 2006.

This book contains a wide variety of games geared to all levels of learners and all four skills. Activities are divided into sections according to the type of game. For each game, it lists proficiency level, skills utilized, amount of teacher control, and time required.

Miscellaneous

Assessment

Burgess, Sally, and Katie Head. *How to Teach for Exams.* White Plains, NY: Pearson Longman, 2005.

This very practical book addresses typical approaches to testing language skills and components, ten golden rules for oral exams, ten golden rules for written exams, strategies for helping students deal with stress, and tasks to prepare students for taking exams. It also includes a guide to all the major international English language exams.

Brown, H. Douglas. *Language Assessment: Principles and Classroom Practices.* White Plains, NY: Pearson Longman, 2004.

This excellent introductory text provides a broad coverage of language assessment. It offers perhaps the most comprehensive, yet easy to understand, introduction to learner assessment currently available.

Tutoring

Dalle, Teresa S., and Laurel L. Young. *Pace Yourself: A Handbook for ESL Tutors*. Alexandria, VA: TESOL, 2003.

For inexperienced or volunteer tutors, this book is an easy-to-follow guide for those who want to tutor individuals or small groups of ESL/EFL learners but do not know how. It includes reproducible forms.

Web Sites

The online addresses for Web sites change frequently, making it difficult to stay up to date with accurate information. If you find that one or more of the following links no longer works, we suggest that you use Google or another search engine to look for the resource with the broken link. Usually you can find the same book or article on the Internet but at a different location.

Exploring Theological English

For additional *ETE* resources, including teaching suggestions, a section on frequently asked questions, and links to relevant Web sites, see the *ETE* companion Web site, http://www.ExploringTheologicalEnglish.com

Vocabulary

The following sites offer resources for teachers and students, including vocabulary tests, learning activities, cloze passage builders, and much more. Most deal with the Academic Word List and the General Service List.

Averil Coxhead's site, http://www.victoria.ac.nz/lals/staff/averil-coxhead.aspx

Compleat Lexical Tutor, http://www.lextutor.ca/

Gerry's Vocabulary Teacher, http://www.academicvocabularyexercises.com/

John Bauman's site (General Service List), http://jbauman.com/aboutgsl.html

Online vocabulary tests, http://www.er.uqam.ca/nobel/r21270/levels/index.html

Paul Nation's Web site, http://www.victoria.ac.nz/lals/staff/paul-nation.aspx

Rong Chang Li's Vocabulary site, http://www.rong-chang.com/vocabulary.htm

University of Nottingham, http://www.nottingham.ac.uk/~alzsh3/acvocab/wordlists.htm

Grammar

Rong Chang Li's Grammar site, http://www.rong-chang.com/grammar. htm

This site lists a number of other sites for teaching and learning grammar.

Pronunciation

John and Muriel Higgins' Web site, http://myweb.tiscali.co.uk/ wordscape/wordlist/

This site offers an extensive list of minimal pairs for British English.

TESOL SPLIS (Speech, Pronunciation and Listening Interest Section) Web site, http://www.tesol-splis.org

This site includes a variety of information and links for teachers and students.

Sites with Links to a Variety of Resources

By accessing the following sites, you can reach dozens of other sites that are relevant for ESL/EFL teachers and learners.

Amity Foundation Teaching Resources, http://www.amityfoundation. org/page.php?page=82

This site offers an excellent collection of practical articles dealing with how to teach various aspects of English, a teacher's toolkit with sample course outlines and a wide variety of teaching materials, links to a range of useful Web sites, and practical advice about living and teaching in China. Even for those who are not teaching in China, this is a superb place for new teachers to gain a good foundation in practical matters related to teaching English.

CAELA (Center for Adult English Language Acquisition), http://www. cal.org/caela/tools/

This site has a large number of free resources for ESL/EFL teachers. Most are short, practical articles for inexperienced teachers and tutors.

Dave's ESL Café, http://www.eslcafe.com/

This is one of the richest sources of TESL/TEFL information on the Internet, including information about jobs, discussion forums, hundreds of links to other Web sites, etc. However, the information you find through the many hundreds of links on this site will vary considerably in quality.

ESL Loop, http://tesol.net/esloop/

This is a collection of sites relevant to English Language Teaching and Learning on the World-Wide Web. Each site is linked to the next, so that no matter where you start, you will eventually make your way around all the sites in the loop.

ICCT TESOL Resources, http://www.wheaton.edu/bgc/icct/

This site includes information about teacher-preparation courses, suggestions for getting started in teaching ESL/EFL, links to other sites, etc.

Sites with a Large Number of Online Articles

The following sites contain a large number of practical articles for ESL/EFL teachers, including teaching methods and techniques, lessons and lesson plans, classroom and tutoring materials, book and software reviews, and links to other Web sites.

CAL Digests, http://www.cal.org/caela/esl_resources/
http://www.cal.org/resources/digest/index.html
English Teaching Forum, http://exchanges.state.gov/englishteaching/forum-journal.html
The Internet TESL Journal, http://iteslj.org/
TESL-EJ, http://tesl-ej.org/

Online Courses

Heinle & Heinle ELT Advantage, http://eltadvantage.ed2go.com/eltadvantage/index.html

More than a dozen practical courses for new and less experienced ESL/EFL teachers.

Professional Organizations

The Web site for the Christian English Language Educators Association (CELEA) includes newsletters, blogs, and other information of interest to Christian educators (http://www.celea.net).

TESOL (Teachers of English to Speakers of Other Languages) is a widely recognized professional association. In addition to the international organization, there are more than 90 worldwide affiliated organizations. Based in the USA, TESOL sponsors conventions, workshops, and other learning opportunities, and it also publishes journals, books, and an electronic bulletin of employment opportunities. Their Web site is a rich resource for TESOL members and non-members (http://www.tesol.org/). See TESOL's Worldwide Affiliate Directory for an up-to-date listing of affiliates in North America and elsewhere in the world.

IATEFL (International Association of Teachers of English as a Foreign Language) is similar to TESOL but smaller in membership and is based in the United Kingdom (http://www.iatefl.org/).

Notes

Introduction

1. When we talk about the term *proficiency* or *language proficiency*, we are concerned with (1) what an individual can do in the language (e.g., read simple English paragraphs about everyday topics) and (2) how well he or she can do it (e.g., understand the most important points, but not all of the details). Several organizations have specified a range of proficiency levels for each of the four language skills—listening, speaking, reading, and writing. However, the names used for each level and the exact ability range represented by each level differ somewhat. Commonly used levels are beginning (or novice), low-intermediate, intermediate, high-intermediate, low-advanced, advanced, high-advanced, superior, near-native. Many ESL/EFL programs do not include a level called superior, but instead have only advanced or high-advanced as the highest level. For more information on proficiency levels, including comparisons of four different proficiency scales, see *TG* Appendix 1, pp. 114–115

2. TOEFL (Test of English as a Foreign Language): An English proficiency test for non-native English speakers who are applying to colleges and universities where English is the medium of instruction (http://www.ets. org/toefl). IELTS (International English Language Testing System): Similar to the TOEFL, this English proficiency test is widely recognized by educational institutions and government agencies (http://www.ielts.org). The TOEFL uses American English and is more popular among those who are applying for admission to institutions of higher education in the United States and Canada. The IELTS uses British English and is more widely used by those who wish to study in the United Kingdom, Australia, and New Zealand.

Unit A: Preparing to Teach *Exploring Theological English*

1. If your students have taken the TOEFL or the IELTS, ask to see their test scores. Those who have low to moderately low scores are likely to find the readings in *ETE* to be too difficult. For this reason, you may want to require these students to continue their study of GPE before studying *ETE*. Or, if they are already enrolled in a class that uses *ETE*, you may want to require them to continue their study of GPE until they reach a higher level of overall proficiency in English.

    A viable alternative for determining your students' English proficiency is to use the sample tests available in TOEFL and IELTS preparation manuals. These practice tests make good substitutes for the TOEFL and IELTS because they are identical in format and length to the actual tests. Most manuals for these two tests also provide a description of the test and information about test interpretation; all manuals provide answer keys. Although the results from these sample tests would not be accepted for admission to a university, they should be sufficient for your purposes. In addition to gaining an accurate assessment of your students' ability to use English in a variety of settings, data from these sample tests can be valuable for pinpointing areas of the language that need improvement. Furthermore, because these manuals contain a number of practice tests, you can measure your students' improvement over a period of time by using one sample test at the beginning of instruction and another after a few weeks or months of instruction. These books can be purchased at most large bookstores in many cities worldwide. They are also available from publishers with Internet sites, such as Pearson Longman, Oxford University Press, Cambridge University Press, and Heinle ELT (see *TG* Appendix 4, pp. 126–133).

2. The Vocabulary Levels Test consists of separate tests to measure knowledge of vocabulary at word levels ranging from 1,000 to 10,000. A number of versions of these tests are in Nation (2001, 412–428) and on Paul Nation's Web site (http://www.victoria.ac.nz/lals/staff/paul-nation.aspx). Also see http://www.er.uqam.ca/nobel/r21270/levels/index.html for versions that can be taken and scored online. These include two versions of the 1,000 word level test and three versions of the 2,000 word level test.
   In addition to the actual Vocabulary Levels Test, Nation's Web site includes some short practical articles about using and interpreting this test.

3. The *General Service List of English Words (GSL)* (West, 1953) consists of about 2,000 word families that appear frequently in spoken and written English. You can find this widely used word list on a number of Web sites including Nation's site (http://www.victoria.ac.nz/lals/staff/paul-nation.aspx).

4. Although studies report somewhat different results, Coxhead (2006, 2) found that the most frequently used 2,000 word families in the General Service List cover about 75% of the words in academic textbooks and about 90% of words in fiction writing. Nation (2001,16) says that the same 2,000 word families represent about 82% of the words in academic texts, with the first 1,000 words covering about 77% of the words in academic textbooks and the second 1,000 words an additional 5%.

5. See http://www.rong-chang.com/vocabulary.htm for a list of Web sites for learning English vocabulary.

6. For more resources for studying academic vocabulary, see *ETE* Appendix 4, pp. 357–361, and *TG* Appendix 4, pp. 126–133. For more information on the Coxhead Academic Word List (AWL), including practice exercises, see

http://www.academicvocabularyexercises.com. Also see *ETE* Appendix 2, pp. 339–344.

[7.] Coxhead's research (2006, 4–7) shows that approximately 10% of the words in academic textbooks are found in the Academic Word List while only about 4.5% of the words used in newspaper articles appear in the AWL. With about 80% of the total AWL vocabulary coming from Greek or Latin, this means that English learners who already know a Romance language will generally find it easier to learn the AWL words than will those who speak languages such as Mandarin Chinese, Arabic, or Thai.

[8.] To read more about Coxhead's AWL and how these 570 headwords were chosen, go to her Web site, http://www.victoria.ac.nz/lals/staff/averil-coxhead.aspx.

[9.] Three additional vocabulary tools are the Range Programme by Paul Nation, the Web Vocabulary Profiler by Tom Cobb, and the Frequency Level Checker by Joyce Maeda. Each of these allows you to determine the number of words in the text that are from each of four frequency levels: the most frequent 1,000 word families, the second most frequent 1,000 word families, the Academic Word List, and words that do not appear on the other lists. Check these sites for other information (e.g., color-coding of the words from each list that appear in your text) and learning activities.

Range Programme, http://www.victoria.ac.nz/lals/staff/paul-nation.aspx

Vocabulary Profiler, http://www.lextutor.ca/vp/eng/

Frequency Level Checker, http://language.tiu.ac.jp/flc/

Appendix 4
[1.] This section, written by Dianne Dow, is adapted from Dickerson and Dow (1997, 44–45).

Appendix 5
[1.] We thank Dianne Dow for her substantial contributions to this appendix.

References

Coxhead, Averil. *Essentials of Teaching Academic Vocabulary.* Boston: Houghton Mifflin, 2006.

Dickerson, Lonna J., and Dianne F. Dow. *Handbook for Christian EFL Teachers: Christian Teacher-Preparation Programs, Overseas Teaching Opportunities, Instructional Materials and Resources.* Wheaton, IL: Billy Graham Center, 1997.

Hutchinson, Tom, and Alan Waters. *English for Specific Purposes.* Cambridge: Cambridge University Press, 1987.

Nation, I. S. P. *Learning Vocabulary in Another Language.* Cambridge: Cambridge University Press, 2001.

Pierson, Cheri. *Dictionary of Theological Terms in Simplified English: Student Workbook.* Wheaton, IL: Evangelism and Missions Information Service, 2003.

Seymour, Sharon, and Laura Walsh. *Essentials of Teaching Academic Reading.* Boston: Houghton Mifflin, 2006.

West, Michael. *A General Service List of English Words.* London: Longman, Green & Co, 1953.

Also available from Piquant Editions:

Exploring Theological English:
STUDENT TEXTBOOK

Cheri L. Pierson, Lonna J. Dickerson, Florence R. Scott

p/b, 396pp, 246x189mm
ISBN 978-1-903689-01-1

Exploring Theological English is a theology ESL/ EFL textbook for high-intermediate to advanced learners of English. It develops:

- key reading skills

- a broad general, and an expanding academic, vocabulary

- skill in figuring out complex grammatical structures

- familiarity with the important concepts and terminology used in theological writing.

www.piquanteditions.com